A CLASSIC CONNECTION

A CLASSIC CONNECTION

The Friendship of the Earl of Derby
and
the Hon. George Lambton
1893–1945

Michael Seth-Smith

SECKER & WARBURG
LONDON

First published in England 1983 by
Martin Secker & Warburg Limited
54 Poland Street, London W1V 3DF

Copyright © 1983 by Michael Seth-Smith

British Library Cataloguing in Publication Data

Seth-Smith, Michael
   A Classic connection.
   1. Lambton, George   2. Derby, Edward
   George Villiers Stanley *Earl* of   3. Horse-racing
   789.4   SF334

   ISBN 0-436-44705-3

Photoset by Rowland Phototypesetting Ltd
Bury St Edmunds, Suffolk
Printed and bound in Great Britain by
St Edmundsbury Press, Bury St Edmunds, Suffolk

Contents

List of Illustrations

Introduction and Acknowledgements

The thoroughbreds owned by Edward Stanley, 17th Earl of Derby, and trained for him by the Honourable George Lambton, dominated English racing for almost thirty years. This domination commenced in the halcyon era before the First World War, continued through an age when social status and tradition ruled the Turf and commercialization was subservient to the aim of breeding and racing top-class horses, and only ended in the 1930s as a result of a quarrel between the two aristocrats which might have been resolved had it not been for misunderstanding and stubborn pride. Happily the two men had the strength of character, the good sense and the heart to settle their differences before the outbreak of the Second World War, and had revived their unique relationship before the death of Lambton in 1945 at the age of eighty-four.

In 1924 George Lambton wrote *Men and Horses I Have Known*, which even today is generally acknowledged to be the best racing autobiography ever published. Although he subsequently wrote newspaper articles on racing and contributed to periodicals, he never updated his life story, although frequently requested to do so. Consequently I was delighted when it was suggested in the spring of 1980 that I should write a biography of the Hon. George Lambton which would emphasize the final two decades of his life. The suggestion took root as a result of my accepting an invitation to stay at Mesnil Warren, the Newmarket home of Teddy and Pauline Lambton. Their hospitality is renowned, and is generously offered amidst a treasure-trove of memorabilia concerning Teddy's famous father. Paintings by Sir Alfred Munnings and Lynwood Palmer, cups, trophies and other racing souvenirs are eloquent testimonies to the distinguished career of George Lambton. In such an atmosphere the thoughts for the biography blossomed.

As the proposed book was discussed in detail it became abundantly clear that the life of George Lambton was so closely linked with that of the 17th Earl of Derby that I should have to make an approach to his grandson, the 18th Earl of Derby, to ascertain if any

additional scrapbooks relating to the famous horses trained by
Lambton at Stanley House were still in existence. Lord Derby, with
typical kindness and understanding, gave his permission for a
search to be undertaken in the hope that previously undisclosed
information, letters or documents might be discovered. The search
exceeded my wildest hopes and dreams, for nine cardboard boxes
were unearthed at Stanley House which contained much of the
correspondence between Lord Derby and George Lambton between 1917 and 1945. Each box contained 100–200 letters, those
from Lord Derby being carbon copies and those from Lambton the
original. An enormous number of these letters referred to trial
gallops, entries, the health of Classic candidates and the purchase
and sale of bloodstock. The remainder gave an intriguing insight
into racing England between the two world wars, and the problems
besetting the most powerful training establishment in the country.
The letters also highlighted the relationship of Lord Derby with
George Lambton and provided sidelights upon contemporary history.

From the moment that I set eyes on those letters I was convinced
that the complexion of the proposed book should be changed,
provided that the 18th Earl of Derby agreed to their publication as
the backbone of it. The fact that he gave his consent without demur
and added to my pleasure by inviting me to Knowsley, where he
gave me further information about his illustrious grandfather, was
generosity that I will never forget. I also owe an immense debt of
gratitude to Teddy and Pauline Lambton for their help, constant
enthusiasm and hospitality; to John Hislop; and to David Farrer,
literary adviser to publishers Secker & Warburg, who sadly died in
March 1983.

Michael Seth-Smith
Magnolia House
Hindhead

1

The Early Career of the "Honourable George"

The Honourable George Lambton, to be known to the entire racing fraternity as the "Honourable George", was born on 23 November 1860. In the Derby of that year, contested six months before George Lambton's birth, both Viscount Palmerston and the 14th Earl of Derby had runners, but neither the Prime Minister's colt nor that which carried the famous "black, white cap" colours of the former Prime Minister finished in the first three – to the disappointment of many of the thousands of spectators who had left the grime, smoke and incessant toil of overcrowded London to enjoy the refreshing air of Epsom Downs. Life was harsh for these city-dwellers, and did not compare favourably with the leisure found in the green and pleasant acres of rural England where feudalism still held sway, and where living was a gracious experience for affluent landowners and their families, who considered hunting an essential part of their existence.

In the north of England one such family was the Lambtons, who had intermarried with the royal line of Plantagenet in the Middle Ages, had loyally supported the royalist cause during the Civil War, and were staunch Whigs who for generations had represented the county of Durham in Parliament after Parliament. They were also renowned sportsmen who owned vast tracts of land, much of it coal-producing. One of the most famous members of the family was John George Lambton, who at one time had been known as the most cantankerous man in the House of Commons, and was created 1st Earl of Durham in 1828. Ten years later he became first Governor General of Canada. He loved fox-hunting; was a fine shot; a first-class judge of a yearling; for many years maintained a large stud farm; and seldom had fewer than three thoroughbreds in training at Newmarket. His eldest son, George Frederick d'Arcy Drummond Lambton, who became 2nd Earl of Durham and who had married Lady Beatrice Hamilton, second daughter of the Marquis of Abercorn, soon after his return from a tour of America and the West Indies, was also an enthusiastic supporter of racing.

The best horse he bred was The Wizard, whom he sold as a foal for 200 guineas. In 1860 The Wizard won the Two Thousand Guineas, was second in The Derby to Thormanby and third in the St Leger, before being sold to the Prussian government for 4000 guineas.

The Earl, who was not despondent over his failure to retain The Wizard for his racing career, was praised by a contemporary writer:

> Somewhat retired in his habits, and only a trifling better, the Earl of Durham runs his racehorses as befits his position and as Englishmen like to see. In politics he has taken little part; and residing on his estates, on which his ancestors have lived without intermission since the time of the Conquest, he discharges the duties of a landlord in a manner that will readily account for the wide influence he has over his tenantry, who are as happy and contented as any in the north of England.

In reality the Earl was a staunch Liberal who hated the French almost as much as he disliked the Tories, and was a shy man with a quick temper. Like all Lambtons "he was outspoken to the point of rudeness, had his strictures on family, friends and the world in general not been delivered with a charm and a twinkle in his eye".*

George Lambton, the fifth of the Earl's nine sons, was born at the time when the Prussian government was negotiating to buy The Wizard. Unquestionably his youthful life and that of his eight brothers and four sisters was contented in the extreme, for their father was both kind and considerate, even though he expected them to be accomplished horsemen and horsewomen. There was never any shortage of horses and ponies at their two country homes of Lambton in Co. Durham and Fenton in Northumberland, and at the age of seven George Lambton was blooded by Lord Wemyss after being run away with on his pony whilst hunting near Fenton. The two sports of hunting and fishing in the River Glen went hand-in-hand for the Lambton children, for they would ride the five miles from Fenton to the river in the morning, their ponies would be put up at a local farm, and after a picnic lunch the boys would gallop home, jumping fences from one field to another instead of opening the gates. Rabbits were hunted with terriers, a small mixed pack of harriers and beagles were kept, and all country pursuits were followed with verve and enthusiasm. It was claimed that "Lambtons are born in the saddle, and ride by the light of nature", and certainly

---

* Comment by William Douglas-Home, contemporary author and playwright.

this was true of young George and his brothers. His eldest brother John had been born in June 1855 only moments before his twin Frederick. Next came Hedworth, followed by Charles, whilst George's younger brothers were William, Claude d'Arcy and Francis.

Although scholastic education and schooling were considered necessary evils by all the Lambton children, George was sent to a private school at Winchester for one term before moving to another preparatory school at Brighton. When he was eleven his mother died, and two years later he went to Edmund Warre's house at Eton. He failed to come to terms with the distinguished scholar who was his housemaster, and in consequence failed to enjoy his Eton schooldays as much as he might have done. Due to his poor relationship with Warre, who insisted that he assiduously improve his Latin even if it prevented the more pleasurable pastimes of cricket and football, George Lambton's record as a schoolboy athlete suffered, and his prowess with bat and ball was never fully recognized. He was discovered returning surreptitiously from Ascot races one summer's evening, and paid the penalty for his transgression by being given a Georgic to write out, but otherwise did not get into hot water during the three almost wasted years that he was at Eton.

Schooldays were followed by months with a tutor at Bere Regis, cramming to pass the entrance exams for Cambridge. As a true countryman he quickly discovered opportunities to hunt with the East Dorset, Cattistock and Blackmore Vale, and to shoot and fish, invariably accompanied by his beloved fox-terrier "Trap", who had been acquired from the Home for Lost Dogs at Battersea. As a result his unfortunate tutor found that this pupil's attention frequently wandered from his work – particularly if the sun was shining! However, the necessary exam result was procured and George Lambton managed to gain admission to Trinity College, Cambridge.

He had little or no intention of working hard at his academic studies at the University, and once he realized that his tutor was prepared to tolerate such a lack of enthusiasm he devoted himself wholeheartedly to those pleasures offered to the sport-loving undergraduate. He became a member of the Beefsteak Club; gained the reputation of being somewhat of a dandy; rode with the Drag, which he found indifferent after the quality of the hunting provided in Durham, Northumberland and Dorset; and watched many of his contemporaries lose more money than they could afford by gambling. This folly put him off gambling in private houses and playing poker or any other card game for high stakes for the remainder of his life.

George Lambton certainly failed to make the most of his days at Cambridge, and after the death of his father he was not sorry to accept the suggestion of his guardian, Charles Barrington, that he should leave and cram for the Army exams. The crammer chosen was the renowned Mr Faithful at Storrington, some twelve miles from Brighton, but eighteen-year-old George had no genuine desire for the life of a soldier. In fact from the outset he showed so little enthusiasm for his work that Mr Faithful told him point-blank that he would tolerate him as a guest but not as one of his seventy pupils. Yet in some respects George was content at Storrington, for the majority of the pupils possessed horses, and in midsummer he organized the Storrington Derby on the Downs above Michel Grove. He won the race easily on St Julian, a hack which was the last present he had received from his father.

Although so young, he already knew exactly how he wished to spend the remainder of his life: the Turf. He had assessed the situation, analysed his own ability, critically considered his love of horses and hunting, and ignored the drawback that by the Turf's current standards he was financially ill-equipped for such a career. He received an allowance of slightly more than £750 a year from family trusts, and although this income would have represented considerable affluence to the majority of men, it was inadequate for his needs. However, from whatever angle he reviewed the situation he invariably arrived at the same answer: the Turf! The problem was to decide how best to go about fulfilling his ambitions. To enter the ranks of owners on a lavish scale was out of the question, and equally he was far from rich enough to set up as a trainer. The thought of becoming an assistant trainer entered his head, but was grandly discarded on the grounds that no aristocrat could demean himself in this manner.

Whilst he was deliberating his future he bought his first race-horse, Burgomaster, who was advertised to be sold for ninety sovereigns in the *Exchange & Mart*. Burgomaster, an ugly four-year-old nearly seventeen hands high, was sent to Fred Barrett, who trained at Findon, only a few miles from Storrington. Within weeks of his purchase George Lambton went to London, impetuously borrowed a thousand pounds from a moneylender at the usual exorbitant rates of interest, and paid £150 to Barrett for another horse, The Martyr, whom he rode in a race at Warwick. His guardian and his tutor would have opposed such an action, so he rode The Martyr in the name and colours of Lord Douglas

Gordon. The horse finished second and was promptly claimed for £200, but the thrill of the race made George Lambton more determined than ever that his career should be on the Turf.

He rode his first winner in October 1880 when he won a race at Nottingham on Pompeia, owned by a burly Yorkshireman, Tom Green, who had once trained for his father, and was currently training for his elder brother, the 3rd Earl of Durham, who had inherited the title and estates on their father's death. To highlight the Lambton love of racing, at the time of George's first success six of his brothers had thoroughbreds in training.

In the course of the next two seasons he rode winners at Sandown, Stockbridge and Croydon, with such renowned gentleman riders as Roddy Owen, Lord Marcus Beresford, Lord John Manners, Arthur Coventry (known as "The Stayer"), Captain S. F. Lee-Barber ("The Shaver"), "Buck" Barclay, Count Kinsky and the Beasley brothers toiling in his wake. It was a glorious era for the amateurs whose exploits in the saddle were matched by their achievements as debonair men-about-town, who were considered suitable escorts for eligible society girls even if there were times when they preferred the company of "Alhambra" courtesans. One of the chasers on whom George Lambton won many races was Bellona, whom he rode in the 1887 Grand National, when the mare came to grief at the second fence. In total he rode in five Grand Nationals, being eighth on Lioness in 1885, then unplaced on Redpath the following year, on Bellona in 1887, and on Savoyard in 1888 and 1889. Savoyard was unlucky in 1888, for he seemed assured of victory at the penultimate fence, but crossed his legs and crashed to the ground, giving his rider a heavy fall. However Savoyard was a useful steeplechaser whom George Lambton rode to finish third in the Grand Steeplechase at Auteuil, a race he won in 1888 on Ronnie Moncrieff's Parasang. He was stony-broke when he arrived in Paris on the eve of the race, and his temper was not improved by the refusal of his friends to allow him to join them in drinking magnums of Bollinger and Krug. On the day of the steeplechase Paris was subjected to a heat wave of tropical strength and by mid-afternoon was sweltering with temperatures in the 90s. George returned to scale in triumph, and one eye-witness commented: "As George – then a really handsome man – rode back into the pesage, the belles Parisiennes assembled there – of the world and half-world – greeted him most effusively. 'Bookays' were thrown at him, kisses were blown from fair hands into his face, and well it was a good job that he was still a bachelor, otherwise 'Mrs Lambton' would have had cause to become exceedingly jealous."

During the next few years George Lambton spent more time on the racecourse than off it. He made the acquaintance of Fred Archer and George Fordham, "swells" such as Sir John Astley and Sir George Chetwynd, and inevitably Sam Lewis, whom he considered the best and straightest moneylender of the era.

When he went to Lewis's London office for the first time he was greeted with the comment: "I have been expecting you for a long time, young man. You have been betting very high and have got no money. What can I do for you?" The desired £1000 was immediately loaned – with the severe caution that the money plus interest was to be returned in three months, or the consequences would be dire. The caution was taken seriously, and the amount repaid, but in subsequent years George Lambton was a frequent visitor to Sam Lewis's office. He was too heavy a gambler not to come to the brink of penury, and pride prevented him from confiding in his eldest brother on every occasion when he was in desperate financial straits.

Eventually the 3rd Earl of Durham, disheartened by George's addiction to gambling, arranged that he should sail across the Atlantic to Canada where his uncle, Lord Lansdowne, was Governor General. The arrangement appalled George Lambton, but luckily he was saved by Sam Lewis having him arrested and sent to prison for non-payment of a debt. He was released after twenty-four hours, having promised not to leave England. It was only years later that he discovered that Sam Lewis had approached Lord Marcus Beresford, who told him that George Lambton dreaded leaving England, and that as a result of their conversation the curiously generous-hearted Lewis deliberately had him arrested to prevent the Canadian trip.

In 1886 George Lambton, Count Kinsky, Baron de Tuyll and several of their friends had sent horses to Joe Cannon at Crafton House, Newmarket. The headache of how to raise the wherewithal to pay the training bills was a perpetual problem, but they managed to survive for several seasons even though their horses were of little consequence. George Lambton was accepted as a familiar and popular figure on the racing scene, acknowledged and admired as one of the best gentleman riders of the era, and was *persona grata* with many of the most influential members of the Jockey Club. It was a halcyon age, with racegoers privileged to see such champions as Isonomy, Ormande, St Simon, Bend Or and Bendigo, ridden by heroes of the skill and artistry of Fred Archer, Tom Cannon and Jack Watts.

In February 1892 George Lambton had the misfortune to suffer a crashing fall in a three-mile steeplechase at Sandown Park. He was thrown clear but landed heavily on his back. Some six weeks elapsed before the serious consequences of the fall became apparent, and during this time he rode in several other races. However, inflammation of the spine set in and he was compelled to lie on his back for several months, pondering the hideous news from his doctors that he should never ride in a race again. Once on his feet and seemingly fully recovered, he was able to lead a normal life, although he was forced to wear a plaster jacket for two years and the injury was to affect his health for the remainder of his life. Understandably he was depressed in addition to being financially very hard-up, but found a little solace in an excursion into racing journalism when he was invited to join Lord Marcus Beresford as the racing expert of the *St Stephen's Review*, which was edited by William Allison.

Nevertheless the months passed wearily and drearily for George until the momentous day when Reginald Brett, later Lord Esher, suggested that he should establish himself as a trainer, and substantiated the suggestion by offering to send him two yearling fillies. There were three objections: firstly, his health was not fully restored; secondly, he knew nothing about training methods and stable management; and thirdly, he was in his usual parlous state of having no money. The latter two difficulties were overcome when his elder brother guaranteed his bank overdraft, Joe Cannon recommended one of his own stablemen to become his head lad, and premises were leased in St Mary's Square, Newmarket. As a result the first objection – the state of his health – was overruled.

Within months he had a dozen horses, several of them owned by Lord Molyneux, son of the Earl of Sefton. George Lambton immediately showed his talent by winning eight modest races under National Hunt rules for Lord Molyneux during the 1892–3 season, and on most of these occasions the owner was the successful rider – much to the consternation of Lord Sefton, who dreaded that his son would suffer as serious a fall as George Lambton had suffered. Their most remarkable triumph occurred on Derby Day, when Isinglass was the hero of the hour – for they, who considered themselves "steeplechasing men", won the second and the fourth race at Epsom.

The previous autumn the two fillies owned by Reginald Brett had been sent to George Lambton as promised. One was a plain angular filly named Hettie Sorrel; the other a useless jade whose career totally lacked merit. Hettie Sorrel finished second in a seller at the first July meeting at Newmarket, and as Fred Rickaby dismounted he advised his trainer that she might improve considerably in the autumn. The jockey's prediction proved accurate, for the filly won three races in succession, thus adding to George Lambton's growing reputation as a trainer. However such a reputation did nothing to add to his bank-balance, and the plain fact was that his financial liabilities far outweighed his assets. Extravagant by nature, and considered by Society as a debonair bachelor whose unusual choice of career was no more than a dilettante whim, George Lambton knew that he must find an affluent and long-suffering patron if he was to continue training racehorses. His overheads were high, and instinctively he realized that there was no guarantee that he could maintain a state of solvency through successful betting. It was as though he was at a crossroads. One path offered nothing but penury and a constant battle for survival if he continued on his own – unless he accepted one of the many suggestions put to him to "marry money". Another path might offer the way to riches, success and comfort – but this path necessitated a rich patron to support him.

It was whilst contemplating the choices offered to him that one summer afternoon he shared a hansom cab with twenty-eight-year-old Edward Stanley, heir to the earldom of Derby, on the return journey to London from Alexandra Park races. He could scarcely believe his ears when Edward Stanley, a man he hardly knew, mentioned that the Stanley fortunes on the Turf were to be revived and suggested that Lambton might be interested in training a number of thoroughbreds on his and his father's behalf. The proposal was manna from heaven . . .

2

The Youthful Edward Stanley

On 4 April 1865 the 14th Earl of Derby, who had been Prime Minister and First Lord of the Treasury on two occasions, was delighted to learn of the birth of his first grandson, soon to be christened Edward George Villiers. When the sixty-six-year-old Earl wrote to congratulate his daughter-in-law upon the arrival of her son, who had been born at Derby House, 23 St James's Square, London, no mention was made of the baby being a potential heir to his earldom and the vast Stanley estates. This omission was understandable; there seemed no likelihood of the baby inheriting the family wealth since his father's elder brother, a thirty-eight-year-old bachelor, was expected to marry and produce children in the fullness of time. Four years later Lord Derby, the renowned "Rupert of Debate", died and within twelve months his successor had married the widow of the Marquess of Salisbury. The new Countess of Derby was forty-five years of age, and from the outset of the marriage there was little probability that she would produce an heir. Consequently as the years passed it became evident that young Edward Stanley would succeed to the earldom of Derby.

Edward's father, Captain Frederick Stanley, had resigned his commission in the Grenadier Guards during the year of his son's birth, and entered the House of Commons as member for Preston. He and his wife, together with the ten children born to them between 1865 and 1878, usually spent the first seven months of each year at their home in Portland Place, London, and the remaining months of autumn and early winter at Witherslack, the 1600-acre Westmorland estate which he had been offered and chosen instead of Ballykisteen in Ireland at the time of his marriage to Lady Constance Villiers, eldest daughter of the Earl of Clarendon.

When Edward Stanley was thirteen he was sent to Wellington College, of which his Derby grandfather had been one of the founders. The decision not to send him to Eton, where so many generations of Stanleys had been educated, had been influenced by the fact that his uncle, the 15th Earl of Derby, had been expelled from the famous school, and in consequence was prepared to denigrate and disparage Eton whenever the opportunity arose to do so. His whims had to be humoured, for he held the financial purse-strings. Despite some disappointment at not going to Eton, Edward Stanley enjoyed his schooldays at Wellington, even though he distinguished himself neither academically nor on the playing fields. In the holidays he found that sport was not totally lacking in appeal and discovered pleasure and delight in beagling. His interest in racing had commenced at Witherslack, where the butler was a keen enthusiast of "the Sport of Kings" and a friend of the local bookmaker. From time to time the butler received reliable stable information and was prepared to pass on these tips to Edward Stanley, who happily gave him a shilling to wager upon the supposed "good thing". Their association prospered, for the horses usually won.

Although other members of the Stanley family may have disapproved of his involvement in betting, few of them, except for the 15th Earl of Derby, could have decried his interest in racing, for the Stanleys had been steeped in the sport for centuries. About the year 1630, James, 7th Earl of Derby, had sponsored a horse race on the Isle of Man, where he was Lord of the Island. The Civil War put an end to this sponsorship, but after the Restoration the Stanleys revived racing on the island, and also on the Wirral, where they gave their patronage to the sport together with the Duke of Devonshire and Sir Richard Grosvenor. A century later the 12th Earl of Derby founded the historic Epsom race which bears his name, and increased the size of his stud farm at Knowsley, the massive ancestral mansion which was the home of the Stanley family, ten miles east of Liverpool.

In May 1882 Edward Stanley was gazetted in the 4th King's Royal Lancashire Regiment. Three years later he was commissioned in the Grenadier Guards, the regiment with which his family had been closely associated for generations. During this period he was stationed in or near to London, and whenever his military duties permitted he led the carefree life of a young bachelor approved by Society. He gambled to a modest degree, and occasionally sent telegrams to bookmakers if he was staying at Knowsley. A footman who saw these telegrams spitefully informed Lady Margaret Cecil that Edward Stanley was losing money betting. She told Edward's uncle, the 15th Earl, to whom horses and gambling were anathema, and the young man was severely reprimanded for his profligacy.

In 1886 Edward Stanley's battalion was sent to Ireland, and

whilst serving at the Richmond Barracks in Dublin he contracted typhoid fever. As an aid to his recovery he was ordered to convalesce by making a round-the-world trip which included visits to Australia and the United States of America. When he was in the New World his father was appointed Governor General of Canada.

Shortly after his return to England, Edward Stanley became engaged to Lady Alice Montagu, youngest daughter of the Duke of Manchester. Her mother, daughter of Count Von Alten of Hanover, was a remarkable woman who had been Mistress of the Robes during the Derby ministry. After the death of the Duke of Manchester in 1890 she was to become the wife of the Marquess of Hartington, who succeeded his father as Duke of Devonshire the following year – thus causing Edward Stanley's mother-in-law to be known as "The Double Duchess".

Edward Stanley and his fiancée were engaged for only three months before their marriage took place on Saturday 5 January 1889 at the Royal Military Chapel, Wellington Barracks. Among the guests were the Prince and Princess of Wales accompanied by Prince Albert Victor and Prince George, and the Princesses Louise, Victoria and Maud. Sadly, Edward's father and mother were not able to attend the wedding, for the duties of Governor General did not spare them the time to cross and re-cross the Atlantic.

The bride was attended by eight child bridesmaids, each dressed in "cherry ripe" costumes of white poult de soie, pale-blue sashes and muslin caps with bows of pale-blue ribbon, and each wearing a double-heart moonstone and diamond brooch which was Edward Stanley's present to each of them. The wedding service was conducted by the Rev. Lord William Cecil, vicar of Hatfield, and the Hon. Richard F. Somerset, a fellow officer in the Grenadier Guards, was Edward's best man. The reception was held at the Duke and Duchess of Manchester's London home in Great Stanhope Street and was attended by the royal party. Amongst the other hundreds of guests were the Duke of Hamilton, the Duke of Bedford, the Marquess of Huntingdon, the Earl and Countess of Derby, Count Kinsky, the Russian Ambassador, Lord and Lady Charles Beresford, Lady Randolph Churchill, Sir William Gordon-Cummins, Mr Alfred de Rothschild and Lord and Lady Esher.

At the reception many of the wedding presents were on display. The Queen had sent the bride a valuable Indian shawl; the Empress Frederick of Germany a ruby and diamond bracelet; the Prince and Princess of Wales a moonstone and diamond brooch. Edward's parents gave a large diamond star to their daughter-in-law and silver plate to their son, the Earl of Derby a diamond tiara and a "substantial" cheque, and the officers of the Grenadier Guards a silver soup tureen.

In March the newly-weds sailed for Canada, where for the next two years Edward served as ADC to his father, who was renowned for his shyness, but equally for his charm, his modesty and his habit of never being in a hurry to go to bed. 1892 was a momentous year for the young couple: their first child, Victoria, was born in June, and a month later at the general election Edward defeated his Liberal opponent in the Lancashire constituency of Westhoughton. He made little mark in the House of Commons, but quickly gained the reputation of being conscientious and of showing particular interest in matters concerning the Army. Outside Parliament he and his wife led a gay social life, were invited to stay with the Prince of Wales at Sandringham, and attended the principal sporting events during the summer. Rumours that Edward had flirted disastrously with betting probably exaggerated his losses out of all proportion and were never substantiated. Perhaps memories of his grand-father's love of racing coloured the rumours, and the thought that one day he might show sufficient interest to revive the Stanley racing empire added to the speculation. However, there was no immediate possibility of Edward Stanley spearheading such a revival, for his financial resources were severely limited.

In April 1893 Edward's uncle, the 15th Earl of Derby, who throughout his life had loathed horse racing, died and was succeeded by Edward Stanley's fifty-two-year-old father, who returned from Canada to take up residence at Knowsley. The estates that he inherited included more than 21,000 acres at Knowsley; 5000 acres around the town of Ormskirk; the Fylde, a 10,000-acre estate east of Blackpool; another 5700-acre estate at Chipping and Thornley some ten miles further east of the Fylde estate; the 10,000-acre Crag estate near Macclesfield, Cheshire; residential and commercial properties in the city of Liverpool; scattered landholdings amount-ing to 11,500 acres in East Lancashire; Witherslack, the 1600-acre Westmorland property where Edward Stanley had spent so many happy months during his childhood; Derby House in St James's Square, London; and the two properties acquired by the 15th Earl – the Witley Park estate near Brook in Surrey and the 620-acre Holwood estate near Beckenham, Kent, which once had been the home of William Pitt, and where under a tree in the garden he had discussed the abolition of slavery with William Wilberforce.

Many aristocrats, including the dukes of Sutherland, West-minster, Portland and Buccleuch, owned infinitely more acres, but much of these vast areas lay in desolate regions of the Scottish

Highlands, whilst the bulk of the Stanley estate was situated in industrial Lancashire. Curiously the earls of Derby never owned land in Derbyshire, taking their title from the Hundred of West Derby in the county of Lancashire.

At the time that the new 16th Earl of Derby inherited Knowsley, the house could not be considered to be either an architectural masterpiece or a house of extreme comfort. Described as enormous and rambling, with eighty small bedrooms and equally small reception rooms – except for a vast dining room – it was a veritable hotchpotch which had been added to by various earls since the end of the Civil War. The furniture was solid but unexceptional, and there were few fine paintings except for a Rembrandt depicting Belshazzar's Feast. The staff included a butler and under-butler; valets and grooms of the chamber; footmen; chefs; kitchen and scullery maids; and the housekeeper, who had at least a dozen housemaids at her beck and call. Outdoors the head gardener had forty men under his command, whilst in the stables were a large number of grooms, some of whom could remember the halcyon days when the 14th Earl had raced on a lavish scale and maintained one of the finest studs in the country.

Originally the Stanley horses had been trained by grooms at Ormskirk and Delamere Forest, but the 14th Earl of Derby elected to send his horses to the famous Malton trainer, John Scott. He frequently had more than twenty horses in training, and between 1842 and 1863 he owned the winners of 205 races, although he never achieved his ambition of winning The Derby. He won the Two Thousand Guineas in 1856 with Fazzoletto, who started favourite for The Derby a month later; the One Thousand Guineas in 1848 and 1860; and The Oaks in 1851. Six years before his death he gave up the Turf to devote his energy and talents to politics and literature. This decision, followed by the total lack of interest shown by the 15th Earl in all aspects of racing and thoroughbred breeding, caused the Knowsley stud to fall into a state of neglect which persisted until 1893. Happily, once the 16th Earl succeeded his brother, it was readily agreed that the Stanley fortunes on the Turf should be revived. The two vital questions were where to train, and who to employ as a trainer. Newmarket, acknowledged as the head-quarters of racing, seemed the obvious answer to the first question, but as to the second the choice was wider, although both the new Earl and Edward Stanley were attracted to the idea of inviting a man to train their horses who was their social equal.

The Fates must have been in benevolent mood, therefore, when Edward Stanley drove in a hansom cab from Alexandra Park races with the Hon. George Lambton, to whom he impulsively put the proposition that he should become private trainer for his father and himself. To his pleasure the proposition was accepted with alacrity. Only afterwards did it occur to him that he had offered Lambton a heaven-sent opportunity for salvation.

3

Forces Are Joined

The association of Edward Stanley and George Lambton commenced in the summer of 1893. It began on a discordant note, due to the uninvited intervention of Ronnie Moncrieff, who, in the words of Edward Stanley, was "a wrong 'un". Moncrieff, brother of three beauties of the era, Georgina Lady Dudley, Lady Helen Forbes and Lady Mordaunt, overheard a conversation between Edward Stanley and George Lambton concerning the commission to buy horses, and promptly went to Newmarket, where he bought three yearlings. He proceeded to tell Edward Stanley that they had been bought on his behalf. The purchase was immediately repudiated, but nevertheless there was a tremendous row, in which George Lambton attempted to mediate. He had more than a sneaking regard for the dissolute Moncrieff, whom he described as "a good rider, a splendid shot, and a cool bold gambler who lived a reckless life, too fast and too good to last".

Once this contretemps abated, the first horse that George Lambton bought for Edward Stanley was Greywell, an old gelding that he acquired from his hunting friend and companion, Count Charles Kinsky. Lambton decided that it would be appropriate if Liverpool was the venue for Greywell's initial race in the Stanley colours, and the chosen race was the Liverpool Plate on 20 July, the first day of the summer meeting. Greywell won convincingly to record the first success enjoyed by Lambton for his new patrons. This victory delighted the Earl of Derby, a man of deliberate and quiet judgement who was very enthusiastic at the thought of the Stanley fortunes being revived on the Turf, even though he was not inclined to race until a respectable interval of time had elapsed since the death of his brother.

Greywell's and other minor victories encouraged the purchase of more bloodstock. Consequently when the new season opened the following spring the Stanley string of horses included three fashionably bred two-year-olds, two of them sired by Derby winners. These colts were acquired from Sir Daniel Cooper, whilst two more yearlings were bought at the Doncaster Sales in September

1893, one costing 800 and the other 480 guineas. The colts purchased from Sir Daniel Cooper proved backward and slow but matured with age, and in 1895 George Lambton rode one of them, Dingle Bay, to victory at Stockbridge. By midsummer it was decided to buy more thoroughbreds, particularly fillies, with the desired intention of reforming the Stanley bloodstock and then reconstructing and extending the Stanley stud. A year later Dingle Bay won the Ebor Handicap at York to give George Lambton his first important winner.

Ten winters earlier the eccentric Duchess of Montrose had removed her horses and those of her husband from Bedford Lodge at Newmarket and taken them across the Bury Road to stables which had been built some fifteen years previously by the Frenchman Lefevre. The Duchess renamed these stables Sefton Lodge, after her second husband's 1878 Derby winner. She also bought land on both sides of the Bury Road from Bedford Lodge to the Old Toll Bar, much of which land had been owned by an ex-Scotland Yard detective who had turned it into a dairy farm. After the departure of the Duchess, Bedford Lodge became the property of Mr Abington Baird, the profligate generally known as "Squire", who squandered his huge fortune before his death in March 1893. Later in the summer Lord Derby leased the premises from Baird's executors and George Lambton moved his horses into the stables, which were thought to be more suitable than those in St Mary's Square.

Shortly after Lambton went to Bedford Lodge he learned that the Duchess of Montrose had announced her intention to sell up all her bloodstock interests. She had added that she would be taking the step with no regret were it not for "poor Griffiths", who had been the best of stud grooms. When Edward Stanley was told this news by George Lambton he wrote to Griffiths telling him that the 16th Earl of Derby was about to re-start the stud farm at Knowsley, and would like him to take charge of it. Griffiths accepted, with the happiest of results for all concerned. He soon revitalized the paddocks, where the grass had become sour and full of weeds, by treating them with liberal dressings of salt, lime, bonemeal and basic slag. For the first three seasons he insisted that they should be used merely to grow swedes, and for grazing sheep, before they were laid down with barley and grass seed. Trees were planted, and new paddocks laid out, in a transformation that took almost five years, and became a monument to Griffiths's endeavour. Another achievement was his advice that the yearling filly Canterbury Pilgrim should be bought at the Dispersal Sale which followed the death of the Duchess of Montrose in 1894. From this acquisition stemmed the entire success of the Stanley racing empire throughout the next half-century.

When Canterbury Pilgrim was put into training, she was promptly criticized for being too small, although it was agreed that she had a good back and loins. Her neck was considered to be too short and her withers too low. In the spring of 1895 when Edward Stanley was elected to the Jockey Club, she did nothing to redeem her reputation and seemed too backward to be given more than a forlorn hope of showing ability as a two-year-old. George Lambton delayed her début until the St Leger meeting at Doncaster, where she was unplaced in the Champagne Stakes. However, her dejected trainer was consoled when another renowned trainer, Robert Peck, told him not to be downcast because Canterbury Pilgrim looked to be a potential stayer, and in his opinion might prove top-class. The spring of 1896 did not immediately bring confirmation of Peck's comment, for Canterbury Pilgrim proved fractious on the gallops, her temperament deteriorated, she became as spiteful as a cat, and at exercise she pulled so hard that it was virtually impossible to restrain her. Then suddenly she began to improve by leaps and bounds, and it was decided to let her take her chance in The Oaks, for which the Prince of Wales's Thais, winner of the One Thousand Guineas, was a short-priced favourite.

On her arrival at Epsom on the eve of the race, Canterbury Pilgrim was in an atrocious mood, covered with muck-sweat from head to toe, and appeared in no fit state to race. It seemed pointless to run her, but by morning she had recovered her composure, and hopes ran high that she might carry the "black, white cap" with credit. No one thought that she had a chance of defeating the royal filly, but this she did with decisive authority, winning by two and a half lengths, although there was little doubt that as she challenged Thais the two fillies almost rolled into one another. The Prince of Wales, hiding his disappointment, was one of the first to congratulate George Lambton on training a Classic winner – but took the opportunity to suggest that Rickaby on Canterbury Pilgrim came dangerously close to the favourite. Turf history may not have been the strongest point of Oaks Day spectators, and many of them gave not a thought to Canterbury Pilgrim's owner, but for a discerning few came the realization that no more fitting man than Lord Derby could have owned the winner, for his ancestor had won the first Oaks, named after his Epsom estate, in 1779, and a year later had been one of the instigators of "the Blue Riband of the Turf". Canterbury Pilgrim's triumph was the first Classic success for a horse carrying the Stanley colours for forty-five years, and repaired the heavily damaged financial state of George Lambton. At the time he was broke, but he took £1000–£80 about his filly's chance, and received a further £1000 as a present from a delighted Lord Derby.

Canterbury Pilgrim failed at Ascot, largely due to her trainer giving Rickaby the wrong riding instructions, but she redeemed this defeat by winning the Liverpool Summer Cup. George Lambton, who still suffered pain from the injury incurred when he took his crashing fall at Sandown, was compelled by an inflamed back to give up training for a few weeks at this moment, and went to Italy to regain his health. On his return he saddled Canterbury Pilgrim to win the Park Hill Stakes at Doncaster after it was decided that it would be unwise to challenge the Prince of Wales's champion Persimmon in the St Leger. Unplaced in the Cambridgeshire, as was the Prince's Thais and Lord Rosebery's 1895 Derby winner, Sir Visto, she ended the season on a high note by winning the Jockey Club Cup.

Lord Derby offered George Lambton the final decision as to whether Canterbury Pilgrim should be kept in training as a four-year-old, and after long and lengthy deliberation he decided that she should be retired and sent to stud at Knowsley. During the next twenty years she gained the reputation of being one of the most influential brood mares in twentieth-century Turf history, even though she had been excitable and irritable whilst in training. John Griffiths once took his son Walter to inspect Canterbury Pilgrim and told him: "My boy, keep that mare in your eye, and you won't go wrong." Despite her bad temper she was utterly courageous and as hard as the finest steel. Before her death she bred seven winners including Swynford, who became the sire of Sansovino and Blandford, and Chaucer, who sired the One Thousand Guineas winners Canyon and Pillion, and who became acknowledged as an outstanding sire of brood mares. When his daughters were mated with Phalaris the result was immensely successful – witness the careers of Fairway, Colorado, Pharos, Pharamond and Sickle.

Once the 1896 season was over, George Lambton again went abroad, staying at Bordighera on the Italian Riviera with his sister, who had married the Duke of Leeds. He had hoped that the warmth of the winter sunshine would improve his health, but by March he still felt listless, and proposed to Lord Derby that he should remain in Italy for another two months even though the racing season was about to begin. He was uncommonly lucky in having Lord Derby and Edward Stanley as his patrons, for no two more considerate or understanding men walked the earth, and they readily accepted

Lambton's proposal. In fact he did not return to Bedford Lodge until the eve of The Derby, and found on his return that the stable was in the doldrums, with a mysterious epidemic affecting all the horses. Not until the summer meeting at Liverpool did a Bedford Lodge-trained winner materialize. The epidemic lasted intermittently for eight seasons, and 1901, 1902 and 1903 were disastrous years for the stable, made worse by a serious outbreak of "pink-eye" in 1903 which left almost every horse lethargic, off form, and virtually useless for the remainder of their racing careers.

As a result of the abject form shown during three years by their horses, Lord Derby and Edward Stanley, advised by George Lambton, made the momentous decision to buy the Sefton stud farm from the syndicate of developers who had acquired it from the executors of the Duchess of Montrose. These developers had quickly appreciated that the deal they had hoped would prove profitable was not as advantageous as anticipated, and were willing to sell the major portion of the land to Lord Derby, who set in motion plans for building the palatial Stanley House stables and a large house for his own use. Many of the innovations and ideas for the buildings were the brain-child of George Lambton, who proposed that ventilated haylofts should go the entire length of the stables, which were positioned so that they had complete protection from the harsh north-east winds which at times made Newmarket so bleak. There was stabling for thirty-two horses, and above some of them were comfortable dormitories for the stable lads.

Once the stable buildings and the elegant Stanley House were completed, Lord Derby and Edward Stanley made the estate their home during Newmarket race weeks, whilst George Lambton took up permanent residence at Stanley House. The contents of his study gave an indication of his taste and career, for there were photographs of horses, dogs and friends, including a portrait of Roddy Owen, with whom he had been on the best of terms until the famous amateur's tragic death in the Sudan; a signed photograph of Fred Archer upon a horse on which he had wagered his maximum (and won!); a shoe of his favourite mare Bellona, on whom he twice won the Croydon Steeplechase; and paintings of Canterbury Pilgrim, Alt Mark and Glasalt, all of whom he had trained to win a Liverpool Cup. There was also a painting of Greywell, the first horse that he had saddled to win in the Stanley colours.

In 1906 Lord Derby gained immense pleasure from The Oaks victory of his filly Keystone II. She was the first Classic winner of his own breeding, and so confidently was her triumph anticipated by George Lambton that he had no hesitation in telling all and sundry that she was fully expected to win. She followed up this success by winning the Nassau Stakes at Goodwood, but was unluckily beaten in the St Leger on ground which had become as hard baked as brick. Later in the season she won at Sandown and Liverpool, contributing greatly towards the £32,926 prize money which enabled Lord Derby to head the List of Winning Owners – a distinction which delighted him and made him believe that the decision to build the Stanley House stables had been utterly sensible and far-sighted. The next season was less successful. Keystone II, kept in training as a four-year-old, was a bitter disappointment, and was largely responsible for Edward Stanley's disinclination in future years ever to keep a filly in training for a third season. Another of his constant aims was to breed horses who could win over a distance of a mile or further, and consequently he never sent his mares to purely sprinting stallions.

Lack of success again dashed the hopes of Lord Derby, Edward Stanley and George Lambton in 1908, and in May tragedy struck the Stanley House stables. George Lambton had been at Kempton and arrived at Newmarket railway station at 10 pm to be greeted with the calamitous news that his stables were on fire. Dashing to Stanley House he discovered that a frantic fight was in progress to save them. The fire had started two hours earlier and had been fanned by a high wind, destroying twenty-five boxes. To make matters worse the majority of the stablemen had gone to a local entertainment, leaving only two elderly men in charge. With presence of mind they unlocked every stable door, letting out the thoroughbreds, but unaided they had no chance of controlling them. Many valuable thoroughbreds galloped free throughout the hours of darkness, but luckily they were all recaptured at first light and returned to temporary quarters, exhausted and bewildered. A few had cuts and bruises, but most were unharmed. When the damaged stables were rebuilt George Lambton insisted upon the installation of fire doors as a safety precaution.

By the time that the fire damage was repaired, the Duke of Portland no longer had horses trained at Stanley House, and besides Lord Derby and Edward Stanley the only other owners for whom George Lambton trained were Sir Horace Farquhar and Captain Hedworth Lambton. However a new and very important character was about to enter George Lambton's life. Her name was Cicely Horner.

4

The Lambton – Horner Marriage

The "Honourable George", although considered a confirmed bachelor, was thought to be one of the most handsome men in Newmarket and was never short of aristocratic female admirers, who included Edith, one of the four renowned Cadogan girls. ★ However he never succumbed to their plans to ensnare him into matrimony. His haughty good looks and charm of demeanour, together with his evident ability as a trainer and his prowess in the hunting field, set many hearts aflutter, yet he continued to retain his freedom. In the summer months he played tennis every Sunday. During the winter he spent every available moment hunting – usually with the Grafton or the Pytchley. He shared a hunting box near Market Harborough with Count Charles Kinsky, and when they rode to hounds it was claimed that "Kinsky was brave to the point of recklessness and that Lambton had the Olympian calm and quiet judgement which showed the perfectly finished rider".

During Ebor week 1908, when George Lambton was staying with Frederick Green at The Treasurer's House at York, he met Cicely Horner, who was also a house guest for the races. Cicely, whose younger sister had married the brilliant scholar Raymond Asquith, son of the Prime Minister, the previous August, made such an impression upon him that he decided to relinquish his bachelor status. He and Cicely became engaged in the autumn and were married on 7 December 1908. In the weeks before the wedding George's eldest brother, Jack, agreed to settle all his outstanding debts. At the meeting between the brothers to finalize the list of impatient creditors, the majority of whom were London tradesmen, Jack asked if the list was totally complete. "Oh," said George, "I believe I also owe a few trifles to some locals in Newmarket."

★ Edith married Lord Hillingdon; Sybil ("Portia") married Edward Stanley; Cynthia married Sir Humphrey de Trafford; Mary married the Duke of Marlborough. Their mother, Mildred, married Hedworth Lambton as her second husband. In 1911 Hedworth was persuaded by Lady Meux to change his surname to "Meux" by Royal Licence, his inheritance of her fortune being conditional upon this. Nothing would have induced George Lambton to do such a thing.

These locals were requested to forward their bills for settlement to the Earl of Durham, who was disagreeably surprised to learn that his brother had run up a bill of £3000 over the years with one grocer who had given him limitless credit in the sublime belief that the account would be settled eventually!

The Horner family, whose ancestral home at Mells had been described as a "small gabled Somerset Manor House, a stone's throw from one of the finest churches in England", had been immortalized by the nursery rhyme "Little Jack Horner", which was a political satire upon Sir John Horner, one of King Henry VIII's Commissioners for the Dissolution of the Monasteries, and a Steward of the Temporalities of the Abbey of Glastonbury. The "pie"★ in the nursery rhyme into which Sir John Horner "put his thumb" was a reference to the Church lands which he took charge of and administered on behalf of the Crown. His prize "plum" was the title deeds to the manor and estate of Mells. He was also mentioned in another mid-sixteenth-century Somerset jingle "Wyndham, Horner, Popham and Thynne; when the Abbot went out, they came in".

Cicely Horner, one of the tallest unmarried girls in Society, was described as "having considerable pretensions to beauty of the statuesque type, straight regular features, very pale complexion, and masses of smooth dark brown hair". She belonged to a group of Society girls known as "The Young Souls", which included Lady Marjorie Manners and Miss Viola Tree, and she was an artist of no mean talent, whose drawings had been exhibited at the New Gallery. She inherited her artistic talent from her mother Frances, who in her youth had been a favourite model of Burne-Jones.

Frances Horner was one of a family of eight – six girls and two boys. Their father, William Graham, was a prosperous merchant with business interests in India, and for many years was one of the three members of Parliament for Glasgow. A Liberal politically, by religion he was a Presbyterian and a strong Sabbatarian. He brought up his children strictly at their home – Langley Hall, near Manchester – but allowed all of them to have ponies. Later the family moved to London, living at first at 54 Lowndes Square and subsequently in Grosvenor Place, where William Graham entertained many of the Pre-Raphaelites, and acquired paintings by Millais, Rossetti,

★ "Little Jack Horner sat in the corner
   Eating a Christmas pie.
   He put in his thumb
   And pulled out a plum
   And said, 'What a good boy am I!'"

Burne-Jones and Holman Hunt. Renowned for his appreciation and knowledge of art, he was appointed a Trustee of the National Gallery in 1884. On Saturday afternoons he used to give some of his children a treat by taking them to Rossetti's studio in Cheyne Walk.

Every autumn the Graham family would go to Scotland, taking Stobhall Castle at the head of the Pass of Killiecrankie as a fishing lodge. For the winter they returned to London, where some of their highlights were the musical evenings spent with the Balfours, the Lytteltons, and the Gladstones, who were usually residing at No. 10 Downing Street. William Graham's wife, an accomplished pianist, had been a pupil of Liszt and Mendelssohn and a friend of Charles Hallé. She instilled a love of music into her children which they never lost.

Frances Graham adored horses, and rode every day in the Row, but she never hunted. More than any of her brothers or sisters, she shared her father's passion for art and artists. In 1878 she met Ruskin for the first time when the famous man was brought to the Grahams' London house by Burne-Jones. A friendship was struck up, and Frances Graham took him to the first performance of Wagner's music in England.

Four years later Frances met thirty-eight-year-old Jack Horner, whom she described as "very tall, very good looking, and quite different from any of the men I had known before. He had an extraordinary well-stored mind, was a first-rate historian and a good scholar, and a thorough man of the world, but a very modest one." He had been educated at Eton and Balliol, where he took first class honours in Law and History. He and Frances were married in January 1883 at St Peter's, Eaton Square, before going to Chidding-fold, where they had been lent a house for the first few days of their honeymoon. Later they went to Rome, where Jack Horner developed typhoid.

The Horners made their home at Mells Park, a large Georgian house with two low wings and more than forty bedrooms, though many of them were unfurnished. The only rooms which were lived in on the ground floor were the circular bow-windowed library, with a magnificent collection of books bound in red morocco; the dining-room, which was crammed with family portraits; and the morning-room – but even these rooms were sparsely furnished, with carpets threadbare and silk curtains faded beyond recall.

Life at Mells was feudal, with the Horner family dominating the village, whose spiritual welfare was looked after by Jack Horner's brother, the Rector of the Parish. He was celibate, vegetarian, teetotal, anti-smoking, anti-sport and anti all amusement, but fortunately for all concerned his influence in the parish until he resigned the living in 1891 was nil. Many of the villagers paid rents of only a shilling a week, and with constant repairs to leaking roofs and other expenses incurred in maintaining the cottages, the Horners were always waging a struggle against debt. Yet somehow they survived, spent much of the winter in London and returned to Mells for the remainder of the year. The shooting was considered as good as at Wilton, Panshanger and Longleat, and an invitation "to shoot at Mells" was coveted.

Jack and Frances Horner's first child, Cicely, was born in November 1883. Twelve months later the Horners temporarily took a house at Guildford in order to be near William Graham, who lived at Oakdene and was dying. Burne-Jones was a frequent visitor, and Cicely called him "Mr Rosey" because he invariably brought bunches of moss-roses from his London garden to brighten William Graham's bedroom.

Within four years of Cicely Horner's birth her sister Katherine and her brothers Edward and Mark were born. Her mother claimed that Cicely "entered into beauty when she entered the world, with large eyes, and a complexion like Rose Red and Snow White. She never cried, and was always happy." As a child she was much quicker at lessons than her sister, and loved dolls, of which she had a huge collection, whilst Katherine was more content to read books. In the summer of 1897 the two girls were taken to Brittany for a holiday, and Frances Horner wrote to Burne-Jones: "We were bathing in a heavenly little bay and Cicely picked up a great long gold-brown sash of seaweed a yard long and danced to the edge of the sea with it. I thought she had walked straight out of a picture of yours to comfort me."

Three years later the Horners let Mells Park and moved into the smaller Manor House. Subsequently, Frances Horner wrote: "I do not know how we all fitted in – six of us and constant friends . . . I suppose the summers were as inclement then as now, but looking back on our summer holidays, they seem to me a vision of constant garden life . . . of long days and moonlit evenings as we set out, and strolled amongst the scented borders." As they grew older a French tutor was employed – until the day that he was discovered teaching them circus tricks by making them lie down on the backs of their ponies and pick objects off the ground whilst cantering. The tutor was replaced by a most capable young woman who taught Cicely and Katherine needlework.

Cicely was undoubtedly the beauty, and John S. Sargent came to Mells to paint her portrait. She always insisted that she wished to marry an actor-manager, but ultimately her choice was very different. However, many years later when her mother wrote an autobiographical volume (1933) she commented: "George Lambton is a man who is more universally beloved than anyone of our time. As a son-in-law he was as perfect as he was in every other relationship in life, and I can give no higher praise." A correspondent who claimed to know George Lambton personally wrote: "As he has inherited none of the irritability and aggressiveness of his grandfather – the first Earl – characteristics which have apparently fallen to the share of the present peer, there is every reason to believe that his marriage will be a happy one."

Lady Horner rented Colonel John Leslie's house in Great Cumberland Place for six months to facilitate the preparation for Cicely's wedding. To some extent these months were overshadowed by the mourning of the Horner family for Cicely's sixteen-year-old brother Mark, who had died of scarlet fever.

Society approved of the Lambton-Horner match, although expressing surprise that "Art" should be associated with "the Sport of Kings", and described George Lambton's decision to become a professional racehorse trainer as bizarre. Nevertheless the fact that the bridegroom was the brother of the Earl of Durham, the Duchess of Leeds, the Countess of Pembroke, Lady Robert Cecil and Lady Anne Lambton, who acted as chatelaine for her eldest brother, endeared him to Society. At the same time the knowledge that he lived at Newmarket and earned his livelihood on the Turf was considered *infra dig* by some social gossip columnists who were at pains to point out that he was a "gentleman trainer" often seen strolling across the Severals with his Pekinese at his heels, and who would go around his stables in the morning dressed in an impeccably cut suit from Savile Row, a flower in his buttonhole and wearing brown and white buckskin shoes.

George Lambton had never been perturbed by the comments of those members of Society who thought it extraordinary that a man of rank and title should demean himself by undertaking a professional career for which the original description had been "training groom" and whose members had attended race meetings wearing the livery of their employers, as did footmen and coachmen. Nor did he give more than passing thought to the realization that he was largely responsible for changing the status of his chosen profession by proving that education, culture, and membership of exclusive London clubs did not preclude a man from fully understanding how to manage thoroughbreds and train them to win races. Admittedly

he was referred to as *Mister* Lambton in the racing reports, whilst
other trainers were habitually assumed to be devoid of a prefix to
their surnames – implying a certain amount of snobbery if not
hypocrisy towards professionalism – but this reference was thought
to be justified due to his elegant figure, quizzical smile, his charm
and his dandyism, allied to the fact that his brother was a peer of the
realm.

Due to family mourning, Cicely Horner had no bridesmaids at
her wedding at St Mark's, North Audley Street, but was attended by
three pages: Hedworth Lambton, a nephew of George Lambton;
David Beatty, a grandson of Mr Marshall Field, the Chicago
millionaire; and Lord Knebworth, son of Lady Lytton. Cicely's
wedding dress was of satin and pearl-embroidered tulle, with a
Flanders lace train originally made for Mary, Queen of Scots, and a
deep cream lace veil woven by nuns for the unlucky Queen when
she was imprisoned in Fotheringay Castle.

Among the immense number of wedding presents that the bride
and groom received were a fine chased ewer-shaped gold cup given
to George Lambton by King Edward VII, who also wrote him a
personal letter of good wishes; a silver bowl from the Duchess of
Devonshire; salt cellars from the Duke of Portland; and a dessert
service from the Countess of Derby. Lord and Lady Rothschild
gave him a silver tea-set and Sir John and Lady Horner, his future
father- and mother-in-law, an antique card-table. Twenty of his
closest friends, all members of the Turf Club, jointly presented him
with a Chippendale sideboard and a dozen Chippendale dining
chairs, and from the Newmarket Clerk of the Course came an
amber- and gold-mounted cigar-holder.

Both the bride and groom let it be known that they appreciated
antique furniture, and in consequence seemingly half the peerage
gave them costly wedding presents of furniture and jewellery.
Cicely received a cabouchon amethyst and diamond circular brooch
from the Duke and Duchess of Connaught, a copy of Spenser's
Faerie Queene in six leather-bound volumes from the Prime Minister, and diamonds from the Duchess of Sutherland, the Duke and
Duchess of Rutland and the Earl of Durham. The Countess of
Derby also gave house linen, whilst her husband gave George
Lambton pearl and sapphire links and his bride a Louis XVI
diamond bow. Mrs Patrick Campbell gave old lace; Mr and Mrs
Herbert Gladstone a breakfast service, as did the Mells game-
keepers; whilst the schoolchildren of Mells gave the works of
Shakespeare and Browning. George Lambton sent Cicely a long
jewelled chain set with diamonds and other precious stones, and a

note, written from 7 Grosvenor Square: "All my love to you
darling Cicely, now and for the rest of my life."

Long before 12.30 pm on the wedding day, huge crowds had
gathered outside St Mark's Church in North Audley Street, for
public interest and curiosity was high to watch the arrival of the
famous guests. The church was packed to capacity with dukes and
duchesses, members of the Cabinet and the Jockey Club, the French
and Russian ambassadors, Mrs Winston Churchill, Miss Lillie
Langtry, Miss Irene Vanbrugh and the Earl and Countess of Derby.
The Countess was wearing "a trailing black dress and a long
black-braided velvet coat. Her black toque being relieved by russet-
red ostrich plumes."

At the last moment Cicely decided, on some superstitious
grounds, to dispense with the lace veil of Mary Queen of Scots, and
a veil of plain lace was hastily procured. Amongst those who
witnessed the newly-weds' signatures in the vestry were the Prime
Minister, Lord Derby, Lord Durham, Lord Marcus Beresford, Mr
Hwafa Williams and Mr Arthur Coventry. There was no reception,
owing to the Horners' mourning for Cicely's brother, and after a
quiet family lunch George and Cicely Lambton left on the first part
of their honeymoon for Coworth Park at Sunningdale, lent to them
by Lord Derby. They spent Christmas at Lambton Castle and early
in the New Year they departed for a tour of the Continent.

Soon after their wedding and return from honeymoon the Lambtons moved into Stanley House. However Cicely did not relish
living so close to "George's work" and consequently Lord Derby
loaned them Mesnil Warren, a large house on the opposite side of
the Bury Road, which he had bought from Sir William Cochrane.
Their life settled down to a routine which included the butler
bringing George Lambton rainwater every morning at 6.45 am.
The rainwater would be placed in a small copper pot by the side of
his bed, and heated by means of a paraffin stove. Once shaved,
George Lambton would go to Stanley House to supervise the
horses.

5

Towards War

Edward Stanley had resigned his commission in the Grenadier Guards in the spring of 1895, and had concentrated upon his duties as a government Whip for the subsequent four years. The outbreak of the Boer War altered this state of affairs. He resigned his government post and set sail for South Africa to take up the arduous task of Chief Press Officer. He returned to England early in 1901 and in 1903 was appointed Postmaster General, with Cabinet rank, under the premiership of Arthur Balfour. Unfortunately in July 1905, whilst speaking on the Post Office Estimates, he said in the House of Commons that "some means should be devised by which there should not be this continued bloodsucking on the part of public servants". The word "bloodsucking" caused Edward Stanley's popularity and prestige to sink like a stone in certain quarters, and although he publicly withdrew the term the damage was done; at the general election in January 1906 the majority that he had obtained in the Khaki Election was destroyed by the Labour candidate in the Westhoughton division. The realization that the heir to the House of Derby had been beaten by an operative carpenter and joiner from Bolton stunned many Lancastrians.

Within two years of this political reverse Edward Stanley became the 17th Earl of Derby on the death of his father, who died peacefully at Holwood on 14 June 1908. The old Earl had been out for a walk on a glorious summer's evening. He came into his study, where he told his wife how much he had enjoyed the exercise, sat down in his favourite chair and died instantly. The new Earl received a gracious letter of condolence from the King, whilst the Prince of Wales remarked in a letter written from Frogmore: "Today at Ascot one heard nothing but kind and sympathetic expressions about your dear father." In his reply Lord Derby commented: "Your Royal Highness so rightly talks of us as a united family. It was thanks to father and mother that we were so, and it won't be Alice's and my fault if we do not profit by the example and do all we can to make mother, brothers and sister feel that though it can never be quite the same, the house is still there."

During his father's lifetime the property at Newmarket had been acquired, and also Coworth Park at Sunningdale, bought in 1895, so that the new Lord Derby inherited estates not only in Lancashire but also in Berkshire, Suffolk and Kent. Shortly after he succeeded his father he sold the family house in St James's Square and bought a mansion in Stratford Place, to the north of Oxford Street, which he named Derby House, and which was used for the next thirty years for social and political entertaining. When quizzed at a later date as to the use of the mansion, Lord Derby replied: "Lady Derby must have somewhere to change when she comes up from Coworth to go to the theatre." One of the most glittering occasions at Derby House occurred on 27 June 1911, a week after the Coronation, when the Earl gave a ball at which five distinguished guests bore the title "His Imperial Highness" and twenty the title of "His Royal Highness".

Six months later Lord Derby was elected Lord Mayor of Liverpool, and enthusiastically plunged into the onerous duties which were required of him. He instinctively believed that the fact that he was the fourteenth Stanley to be elected Lord Mayor of Liverpool since 1568 necessitated his giving his wholehearted energy to the administrative, charitable and social duties involved. He became immensely popular, was described as a "real live Lord" by a trade union official, and thoroughly deserved, as he settled to his new tasks, the sobriquet "the Uncrowned King of Lancashire". He was also a personal friend of King George V, who suggested to him that it would be a good idea if the Prince of Wales and Edward Stanley, who were the same age, were to go to Magdalen College, Oxford. In a letter to Lord Derby the King wrote that both he and the Queen were delighted that Edward Stanley and the Prince might become friends and added: "I only hope that my boy will get on with and be as fond of your boy as I am of you."

At this period of his life Lord Derby had a bluff manner, and a faint trace in his accent of the Lancashire brogue. A man full of bonhomie, he was outstandingly conscientious, and perpetually put "service before self". Yet he could be stubborn in his views and opinions, although he never allowed personal rancour to colour his judgement. If he had a fault it was that he was inclined to "run with the hare and hunt with the hounds" in his political life – an inclination which brought him the unfair nickname of "the genial Judas". Certainly he looked genial, for he was physically a robust man, with ruddy cheeks and large frank eyes which gave him an almost boyish look. His favourite reading was extracts from the Bible and the *Sporting Life*. He was supposed to have had three ambitions – to win The Derby, to become Lord Mayor of Liverpool, and to be Prime Minister. He never achieved the last of these three aspirations, for in some respects he lacked the toughness of character which premiership required and was inclined to "blow hot and cold" and to be swayed by the opinion of others. However he never shirked responsibility, although there were occasions when the taking of decisions proved irksome and embarrassing, for such decisions necessitated "plumping" for one side or another. His wealth and influence made all things possible for him, but did not prevent him from disconsolately remarking on one occasion: "I own many houses, but have no real home."

After his father's death, the racehorses of the 17th Earl raced in the name and colours of George Lambton's eldest brother and continued to do so until Royal Ascot 1909, when they once more carried the Stanley "black, white cap". Other owners at Stanley House were now Lord Wolverton, whose wife Edith was to remain one of Edward Stanley's greatest friends throughout his life, Sir Edgar Vincent (later St Viscount d'Abernon) and Mrs Arthur James, daughter of the Hon. George Cavendish-Bentinck MP and a personal friend of King Edward VII.

The Lambton-trained horses did poorly in 1909, but 1910 was infinitely more successful, due to the triumph of Swynford, by John o'Gaunt out of Canterbury Pilgrim. When he first went into training Swynford was "all legs and wings" according to George Lambton, but he quickly showed that he was a colt full of courage and exceptionally good-tempered. He did not seem to mature until the midsummer of his three-year-old career, and was unplaced to Mr "Fairie" Cox's Lemberg in The Derby. He then proceeded to win the Hardwicke Stakes at Royal Ascot, the Liverpool Summer Cup and the St Leger, a victory which George and Cicely Lambton celebrated by buying green Sunbeam bicycles which were used to bicycle to and from the stables and their farm adjoining the Fordham road. As a four-year-old he won the Eclipse Stakes at Sandown, and the Princess of Wales Stakes on the July course at Newmarket. During September he smashed a fetlock joint during a training gallop, but miraculously was saved due to the skill of the famous veterinary surgeon Mr Livock, and in 1913 was sent to Lord Derby's stud, where he became one of the most successful sires of the twentieth century, with his progeny Sansovino, Tranquil and Keysoe winning Classics for Lord Derby; Saucy Sue for Lord Astor; and Bettina for Mr Walter Raphael. In addition his brilliant son, Blandford, became the sire of Classic winners Trigo, Blenheim, Windsor Lad, Bahram, Pasch, Campanula and Udaipur.

Whilst Swynford was giving so much pleasure to Lord Derby by winning the St Leger, his two-year-old Stedfast was also giving promise for the future. In 1911 Stedfast, sired by Chaucer, ran second to Mr Jack Joel's Sunstar in both the Two Thousand Guineas and The Derby before winning two races at Ascot within the space of twenty-four hours. The 1912 season showed that Stedfast had become an immensely good horse, and his six victories included the Coronation Cup at Epsom and the Hardwicke Stakes at Ascot. He was unlucky to be beaten a short head by Prince Palatine in the Eclipse; many spectators thought that Lord Derby should have lodged an objection, but he refused to do so.

During the summer Lord Derby made it clear to George Lambton that he was prepared to help financially if any Stanley House stablemen needed help in case of sickness, and he arranged for an initial sum of £50 to be set aside for this purpose. He also authorized George Lambton to arrange for Mr Lynwood Palmer, the well-known equestrian artist, who was an expert upon the treatment of horses' feet, to be paid a fee to examine those horses in the stable who were suffering from ailments of the foot.

After Stedfast's Ascot victory Lord Derby had sent George Lambton £100 as a present and a similar sum to jockey Frank Wootton. He also told George Lambton that if he ever wished to give up Mesnil Warren and the house was sold, then any moneys over and above what the Trustees had paid for it should be paid to him as a "set-off" against any expenditure he might have incurred on the property.

Throughout the next two seasons, horses carrying Lord Derby's colours won fifty-one races, but none of them was of any great significance, and at the outset of the First World War he had less than thirty horses in training at Stanley House. In the early months of the war he took over the chairmanship of the West Lancashire Territorial Association. A year later the Prime Minister, Mr Asquith, appointed him Director General of Recruiting after Lloyd George had described him as "the most efficient recruiting sergeant in England". The successful manner in which he carried out his duties as Director General led to his appointment as Under Secretary and then as Secretary of State at the War Office – although Haig and Robertson advocated his appointment on the grounds that they wanted a figurehead who would not attempt to override the CIGS.

Haig once commented: "Lord Derby is a very weak-minded fellow, I am afraid, and, like the feather-pillow, bears the marks of the last person who has sat on him!" In another entry in his diary he wrote: "Derby is a nice gentlemanly fellow. I can't think how he can get through his work if he wastes so much time talking on matters of secondary importance." Perhaps this second remark of Haig's contains a clue to Derby's success as a diplomat, and has a bearing upon a letter that Lord Derby, always a prolific letter-writer, wrote to the Prime Minister at the time of his appointment as British Ambassador in Paris in April 1918: ". . . in my wildest moments I have never looked upon myself as a diplomat, but it may be that in my new capacity I shall be in a position to render service to the Army with which, both in peace and war, my whole life has been bound up." This loyalty to the Army was highlighted at the end of the First World War by his efforts to employ at Knowsley and his other estates only those men who had served at the Front. He even admitted that if two men came to him for a farm, and only one of them had been at the Front, then he would get the farm. Although he was patriotically biased in this respect, he was totally unbiased where his relations and friends were concerned, and never exercised any influence to secure nominations, either political or commercial, for them.

Meanwhile at Newmarket George Lambton soldiered on with a depleted staff. His attitude to his horses was in a way like his attitude towards people. Each had its own personality and individuality, good or bad, and was treated with respect. He would never tolerate roughness by others towards a horse and he would not allow his stable lads, when riding out, to jab a horse in the mouth or not pay attention to what was going on. A failure, on some rather difficult ride, to keep their hands down would bring a quick reprimand or some other sign of displeasure.

In February 1915, after Cicely had gone to stay with friends in Malvern, taking the children, Nancy and John, he wrote to her:

> I am so sorry that I forgot Nancy's birthday . . . I am so glad that John has had his first hunt – he evidently understands the theory of hunting and will not confuse it with steeplechase riding, as so many young people do – I am interested to hear that you have been with the Ledbury – that is a most respectable old-fashioned hunt, and I am glad that they continue to show good sport . . . it is a funny thing about French,* it reminds me of Sir Charles Dilke – only his ladies were called Fanny and Eliza . . . You might buy something for Nancy with the enclosed. Your mother has gone to the South Kensington Museum and I do not know what to get . . .

* Sir John French.

A few days later George Lambton received a sad pencil-written letter on cheap notepaper from Charles Kinsky, who had been compelled to return to Austria. He wrote that it seemed easier to get letters into Austria than out of the country, commented upon the tragic death of George's brother "Pickles", and asked the pertinent question: "What made him go out, having his business to look after at home?" Kinsky had always liked Lambton's brothers Billy and Charles more than Hedworth, and caustically inquired: "How are Billy and Charlie? I expect that they are both out whilst Hedworth is tied down by his command at Portsmouth." He did not imagine that the war would last long, and told George Lambton not to enter his colt Whitefield for any races during 1915 until the war was over! He ended his letter: "Bless you, dear old George. Whatever happens we two will always remain the same friends as ever. That I am quite sure of. I have gone through a great deal and I am quite ready to go through a great deal more to the very end – but the cold up here in this terrible country is beginning to get very trying."

George Lambton's youngest brother had been killed in action in October 1914, many of his younger friends had been called up, and so too had Stanley House stablemen and other Newmarket acquaintances. A letter he received from France in March 1915 stated:

> I have been following the racing question very keenly – I do not mind if they do not have Ascot, and rather think that it would be a good thing to abandon, as it is, – after all – more or less a Society function, but I think it is wrong not to hold The Derby – if only for the Stud Book – but I would hold it at Newmarket and other races (I mean the Gold Cup, Hunt Cup, etc.) of Ascot I would dot about the place . . . I think it is splendid that you have taken command of the Newmarket volunteers, and am sure you are doing well. After all it is personality which counts in these things . . .

During the war years, the curtailment of racing precluded success on a grand scale for George Lambton, who had one superlative filly, Diadem, in his yard. Bred by Lord d'Abernon, Diadem won the 1917 One Thousand Guineas, and during a racing career which spanned six seasons won twenty-four races. A filly with the sweetest of temperaments, she was so highly regarded by George Lambton that he christened his daughter Sybil Frances Mary Diadem Lambton. Lord d'Abernon was very superstitious, and whenever one of his horses was successful he had a brooch made with its name in diamonds and gave it to a lady friend, believing that whilst the brooch was worn the horse would continue to win. The brooch made to commemorate Diadem's victories was lost on the lawn at Ascot, and within an hour the filly suffered her first serious defeat.

Throughout Diadem's racecourse career both her owner and trainer were constantly criticized for their determination to subject her to an arduous campaign season after season. In the press she was described as a gallant mare who had been run to death, but such a description was nonsense, for she loved racing, and Lambton and Lord d'Abernon would have taken her out of training immediately she showed signs of exhaustion. Towards the end of her career Alfred Munnings was commissioned to paint a portrait of her.

In July Lord Durham praised Lord Derby for the part that he had played in persuading Lloyd George to agree to the recommencement of racing, and added: "Lord Derby has not allowed his sympathies with the Jockey Club to influence him to disregard his duties as Secretary of State for War." A sidelight on the patriotism of Lord Derby was that during the war he allowed one of his favourite thoroughbreds, Seaton Delaval, to be "called up". The horse earned for himself the Mons ribbon for services rendered in France. George Lambton was also feeling patriotic. In March 1917 he wrote to the editor of *The Times*:

Sir, – Lord Robert Cecil, speaking in the House of Commons, asserts that football and horse-racing are on exactly the same footing. I am curious to know how he arrives at this conclusion. Football is played with a ball and 22 strong and sturdy young men. Racing is played with horses, ridden by small men, the majority under 8 st. and never more than 9 st. A football when its day is over is useless. Racehorses when they can no longer race, if they have proved themselves on a race-course to be sound and good, retire to the stud, where, as stallions or brood mares, they continue the stock of the English thoroughbred, which forms the foundation of horse breeding in this country, and from which have come those horses that, in the earlier stages of war, rendered such invaluable service. To be a good football player you must be big, strong, courageous, active, and alert, all the qualities you look for in a soldier. To be a good jockey, you require these qualities, except that instead of being big, you must be small – no one can be a jockey who weighs over 9 st., and a large majority weigh very much less. Consequently they are not fit to be soldiers.

If there was no racing a great many people who are unfitted for other employment would be thrown out of work; can anyone say that the same result would arise if those professional football matches did not take place? If professional football matches were not allowed, it would not stop football; and there can be no one who wants to stop it when played as a game – but if race-meetings are stopped, the whole machinery comes to a standstill, and needless loss is caused to everyone connected with it. The arguments for the continuance of racing are many, there are also arguments against it, and for which we most of us have sympathy, but the former outweighs the latter considerably, and I can say from my own personal knowledge that many owners of race-horses, had they simply studied their own inclinations and convenience, would have shut up their racing establishments at the beginning of the war.

> Yours &c.,
> GEORGE LAMBTON

In May 1917 Lord Derby's son Edward became engaged to "Portia" Cadogan, and the wedding took place two months later. His twenty-three-year-old daughter Victoria had married Neil Primrose, younger son of Lord Rosebery, two years earlier. When Neil Primrose was killed on active service in Palestine in November 1917 Lord Derby was shattered. He wrote to a friend, "Neil was one of the most lovable men I have ever come across, and one cannot but feel the glory of his death, an example to many men of his age who ought to be fighting, but let Parliament or other shield save them from doing so."

George Lambton and his wife also suffered personal grief. Shortly after arriving in France in 1915 with the 18th Hussars, Cicely's twenty-nine-year-old brother Edward was dangerously wounded by a bullet in the stomach which penetrated his liver and kidneys. His mother insisted on travelling across the Channel to see him in hospital, and wrote to Cicely from Bailleul on notepaper headed "16 Lower Berkeley Street" – her London home – writing across the address "don't say we are here!":

> We got to St Omer, and as we were getting our permits a message came from H.Q. to tell us to go there. We saw Guy Brooke and Billy Lambton – the latter was very angry that we had been allowed up and scorned the notion that we could stay here, but luckily I had a written permit from the A.G. to stay until tomorrow. . . . Edward is very seriously wounded, and, oh darling, the conditions are the most awful ones. A ward full of

wounded and dying – groaning and coughing – just little sort of
bathing boxes with iron beds and very coarse appurtenances and
a few very overworked nurses, last night six hundred came in,
they were lying on stretchers everywhere. . . . The shells are
going on virtually all the time. . . . I do not know how to leave
Edward in these awful conditions.

Subsequently Edward Horner's sister, Katherine Asquith, the
Duchess of Rutland, Lady Diana Manners and the eminent London
surgeon, Sir Arbuthnot Lane, all visited him in hospital in France,
but Cicely Lambton was unable to do so.

Edward recovered from his wounds, and then served in Egypt
for some months, in a post obtained for him by Lord Birkenhead, in
whose Chambers he had worked on leaving Oxford. However he
became bored by light duties and the tedium of office work, and
returned to the Western Front. There he died in November 1917 as a
result of wounds received in fighting near Bois-de-Neuf. At Eton
and at Balliol his friends had included two Grenfells, Raymond
Asquith and Charles Lister, all of whom were also killed in the war.

At the end of hostilities an equestrian statue, *The Cavalry Sub-
altern* by Alfred Munnings, was erected in the church at Mells in
Edward Horner's memory, whilst a War Memorial designed by
Sir Edwin Lutyens was erected to honour the fourteen men, including Edward and his brother-in-law Raymond Asquith, from the
village who had died for England in 1914–1918.

Two years after Neil Primrose's death his widow married Malcolm Bullock, a young Scots Guards officer who was acting as
Military Secretary at the British Embassy in Paris where Lord
Derby had been appointed Ambassador. The reasons for Lord
Derby's appointment were that in the late autumn of 1917 Lloyd
George decided to dismiss both Earl Haig and Sir William Robert-
son, and anticipated that if he took this course of action Lord Derby
would resign from the War Office. In an astute effort to minimize
the furore that this resignation would cause, he proposed that Lord
Derby should go to Paris as British Ambassador.

Lord Derby arrived in Paris in April 1918 and remained as
Ambassador for two and a half years. He spoke little French, but his
energy and enthusiasm quickly made a very favourable impression
upon his French hosts, who saw in him their exact idea of an English
milord. They were also amused by his claim that the only reason
why he had been offered the job was that he neither spoke French
nor was a diplomat. His wife was worried about her German
ancestry and did not join him for several months, but once she did

so she immediately won the hearts of those Parisians with whom she came into contact, particularly those in literary and theatrical circles.

6

The Post-war Years

In the spring of 1918, within days of Lord Derby taking up his new post in Paris, George Lambton won the One Thousand Guineas for him with Ferry, sired by Swynford out of the mare Gondolette, which Lord Derby had bought from Lord Wavertree. Lambton thought that Ferry would have a great chance in the New Oaks Stakes, but admitted to Lord Derby: "I should fancy that Stoney Ford [also trained by Lambton] is better than Ferry, but I have never tried them. . . . Gainsborough is a really nice horse and will probably win the Classic race." In consequence Lambton decided not to run Ferry against him in The Derby but keep her for The Oaks, but before the race she seemed to train off.

When The Oaks was run early in June, on ground which was very firm due to weeks without rain, it proved an unsatisfactory race, with Stoney Ford passing the post ahead of My Dear ridden by Steve Donoghue, and Ferry ridden by "Brownie" Carslake in third place. Donoghue lodged an objection to Stoney Ford on the grounds of bumping and boring, and this was sustained. Disconsolately Lambton explained to Ferry's owner:

> We had an unlucky week, especially for Swynford, for Stoney Ford was far the best mare in The Oaks – but as an objection was made the Stewards had to disqualify us – Martin undoubtedly crossed My Dear but he had her well beaten at the time. He just lost his head. I was very sorry for Venetia James who had come down. Ferry got a lot of bumping and made up a lot of ground up the hill. I do not think that the course suited her too well . . .

Nevertheless, Ferry was a Classic winner, and Lord Derby commissioned Lynwood Palmer to paint a portrait of her, but at the same time he explained to Lambton regarding the Thousand Guineas result: "I am afraid I cannot give quite as much as I did on previous occasions as expenses are so very high and with such limited racing there is little chance of making both ends meet. I am therefore sending you £100 and £50 to be divided amongst the stable and £50 for Carslake. As he gets a percentage he will not do so badly."

George Lambton, always a patriot, had other matters on his mind at the time, for urgent appeals were being sent out from the War Office for volunteers for the East Coast, and as he explained to Lord Derby:

> It is quite impossible for me to ask my fellows to do what I am not willing to do myself, and so I have to offer myself with the fervent hope that they will not take me. If they do it means going at once for two months. The horses are in pretty good shape now and Joe Cannon will carry on alright, most of the training has been done, although they want to be kept healthy and sound – but it is a great nuisance and I hate the idea of it. However I think you will see that there is no escape from it so far as offering to go if I am any use . . .

Although Lambton thought that Joe Cannon was honest, steady and careful, he also considered that, like all Cannons, he was obstinate and rather stupid.

Lord Derby replied to George Lambton:

> It disturbs me very much the idea of your having volunteered to go to the East Coast and to put it quite frankly I do not think there was any necessity for you to do so – at all events I wish you had asked me before you did it. You say that the horses only require keeping in good health and that most of the training has been done but nobody knows better than you do that Joe Cannon is not the sort of person one can trust to do that, quite apart from his having been, as you told me in London, in bad health. The amount of racing is limited and the horses naturally require a lot of training. Of course now that you have done it it is done and there is no getting out of it but I think it is very hard on me and I really think that if you go we must try and get somebody else to look after the horses in your absence.

Weeks earlier the Germans had begun an offensive and shelled Paris, but in his reply to George Lambton Lord Derby remarked:

> The big offensive has begun and I am sorry to say has gone only too well for the Boche. However I hope they will stop the advance though they have got unpleasantly near to Paris. Bertha is not a pleasant thing to have firing and I am told they have got a

lot more of these big guns coming on. They certainly have got two if not three firing now and two of the shells must have gone right over this house and they fell about 600 yards away. The French are not nearly so frightened of the gun as they are of the Gothas and we have plenty of visits from them.

Fortunately he was able to write again a fortnight later:

Things are quieter here now, and though I think that the Italian front now gives some cause for concern and anxiety, it looks as if the Austrians have failed in their big attack, and if they do fail and lose a great many men I do not believe even Germany can keep her in the War.

In fact Lambton did not go to the East Coast as a volunteer, for he was laid low with nettle-rash and eczema from head to foot. He was despondent over the future of Phalaris* – "they have made the weights impossible for the July Cup; he has to carry 11.0 st. – I think that it is quite wrong in old established races like that to make special conditions to stop one horse" – and equally depressed over Swynford – "there seems to be a curse at the moment upon the stock of Swynford, both in training and at stud – let's hope it has all come at once and will end quickly." He also thought that at least one of the Jockey Club handicappers was too harsh, and told Lord Derby:

The man is so bad as a handicapper that for the life of me I do not know if it is incompetence or a deliberate wish to overweight our horses; anyhow with Jersey as Steward and you away I am certain that I should get the worst of any move I made on your behalf. Jack† is, I believe, engaged in a battle at this moment – certainly his poor horses have been most abominably treated and he made a complaint in July . . . there is not the slightest doubt that there is a widespread and strong feeling that the Jockey Club is too much aloof and out of touch with the racing world, and I do not think that it can be wise to ignore this feeling . . .

Lord Derby replied (24 September 1918) from the British Embassy in Paris:

Alice tells me that you think that our horses are very badly handicapped. Of course from a distance it is very difficult to tell

---

* Phalaris won fifteen races at Newmarket 1915–18 and was to prove one of the most prepotent stallions of the era.

† The Earl of Durham – George Lambton's elder brother.

that. I see that the weights they are given are very high but of course that may be nothing. The handicap must be taken in relationship with other horses. If you could give me any flagrant examples of bad handicapping of our horses I will write to the Stewards about it, as it seems to me possible that a dead set may be made against the bigger stables by the handicappers in order to give what they are pleased to call the small men a chance. If that is the case the sooner the Stewards are informed that the bigger owners are not going to stand it the better.

I am afraid racing is going to be extremely difficult next year but the fact that the French are allowing their trial races will I think to a certain extent put a spoke in the wheel of those who are protesting against racing at all in England. At the same time there is no doubt an argument which is a very plausible one although a ridiculous one, namely shortage of forage, and I am afraid that in France there is an unusual shortage of oats and hay and apparently the harvest at home, with all its splendid promise, is going to end by being middling if not a bad one. We have had bad weather here but nothing like what you have had in England. I wonder under these circumstances whether it would be better not to cover any of our young mares and perhaps give some of the older ones a rest? I suppose a mare would do better on what she could pick up if she is not in foal than if she is. You might talk this over with Walter. Of course by next February we shall know better how things are going and here at all events the opinion is the War cannot possibly last more than another 12 months. I do not feel so sure as though I think it is possible Turkey, Bulgaria and even Austria might give way, Germany with her back to the wall will fight like a tiger.

Lord Derby had his own views on the subject of the future of racing, and told George Lambton in December:

It is quite evident that in one way and another the Government mean to crush the industry of horse breeding. First of all by what you tell me about the forage – I do not see how we could possibly go on racing under the conditions you name – and now apparently there is to be a luxury tax on racehorses and on their value, though how that is going to be discovered until they have raced I do not know, and the tax to be as high as 2d. in the shilling. Under these circumstances there is no possibility of going on racing – at all events in England. In India however they are apparently very keen about racing. Patiali was here yesterday and had luncheon with me. He wants to buy something that would have a good chance of winning the Viceroy's Cup and he remembered that his father had bought Sprightly from us. He therefore asked me to write to you and ask if you knew of anything that might be suitable. He won't buy through ordinary dealers and I am afraid amongst the latter he includes Marcus Beresford and Co., but he would like to buy privately and of course would give a Commission. Do you know of anything at the present moment that would be in any way suitable?

Lord Derby was also determined to assist the revival of French racing once the war was over, and he explained to Lambton:

I am perhaps going to buy a couple of yearlings here. They are going very cheap and I am going to get old Dubos to take them into his stable and look after them for me. I spoke to the old man about it today and he seemed most awfully pleased and I know he would do his level best for one. It is just as well to have something in a French Stable because after the War, when racing begins again here, I should want to send some of our horses here and a local trainer would be of great assistance to you when you brought the horses over.

In this letter he added a paragraph about twenty-four-year-old Fred Rickaby, who had been only eighteen when he became stable jockey to George Lambton in 1912, succeeding his father, who had ridden Canterbury Pilgrim to victory in the 1896 Oaks. Towards the end of the war, having won the One Thousand Guineas on Vaucluse in 1915, Canyon in 1916 and Diadem in 1917, Rickaby had joined the Royal Tank Corps.

Poor little Rick. It was very sad indeed his death. I had no idea that he was even in France and if I had known he had been wounded I would have tried to have got up to see him. I am glad to hear from you that his wife and two little children are left fairly well off. I had written to Alice to say if there was any difficulty I should like to help.

Subsequently Lord Derby wrote (4 November 1918) to Lambton about a jockey for the 1919 season:

Do you think any arrangements could be made to secure Carslake now that poor little Rickaby has been killed – otherwise I should have kept the place open for him. I do not myself believe that racing next year can become normal and I very much doubt if we shall have more than we have had this year although there may be a certain extension. All this of course is supposing we have Peace. . . .

Now with regard to another question. I wrote to you on October 9th saying that I felt as Ferry's win in the 1,000 was rather a fluke her picture was therefore hardly worthy to be hung in the Jockey Club in Paris. I therefore asked that the second picture by Lynwood Palmer should not be proceeded with. Was anything done in this matter? I ask because I have got a bill for two picture frames which makes me think he may have painted two pictures.

Lord Derby felt so strongly about having a top-class stable jockey retained that he brought the subject up again in a letter written before Christmas:

With regard to a jockey from what you say there is such a scarcity of jockeys that I almost think it would be better to have second claim on Carslake, if we can get it, rather than try and get anybody else as first string. You are so extraordinarily good at training Jockeys that I feel probably you will find a good apprentice and as I told you if you want me to have one or two selling platers just to help to make him I have no objection whatever to keeping them . . . With regard to Carslake, if you could arrange it what I should like to do would be to give him £1,000 a year for second claim for myself alone, without any percentage per race, but if you think he won't take that I would be ready to go to the extent of 5%. I think 10% seems too high although I quite understand that it might not be too high if he rode for the whole of the Stable, but as you say I do not suppose any of them would contribute much and I do not quite see why I should think of anybody except just myself in this matter.

Before the end of the season George Lambton was convinced that the two-year-olds were mediocre, both at Stanley House and in other Newmarket yards. He was also convinced that 1919 would find him short of horses and overstaffed, for he believed that many of his stablemen who had been called up would wish to return to their former jobs. He explained his views to Lord Derby and added:

I am delighted to hear about your French yearlings. I think you

will have more fun racing in France than here next season. What
with the training grounds here and the difficulties of good forage
we have a poor chance against the country stables who can do
what they like.

Lambton was also perturbed about retaining a jockey:

There is no chance of getting first claim on Carslake. He sticks to
Persse whatever anyone might offer. There is no other jockey
that I think is worth much except Donoghue and you cannot get
him.★ I think that young Colling† might be worth taking on, he
looks to have the making of a first class jockey. His father is away
but I will talk to him when he gets back . . . I hope to get Osgood
back soon he is in the Army Veterinary Corps at Canterbury and
says that he has nothing to do except look after his officer's hacks
since he left me.

By December Lambton was unhappy about the entire future of
Newmarket, particularly as there had been a government enquiry
into racing's headquarters. He wrote to Lord Derby in Paris:

I am going to send you a correspondence with Selbie of the Board
of Trade which I think will answer you. They have fairly given
themselves away and we have a real good case to fight. He sent a
detective down here who has given him a most absurd and
libellous report on Newmarket trainers – the man was as inaccurate as he was ignorant and Selbie swallowed it. I feel very
gloomy about the prospects for Newmarket, the training
grounds are not only getting smaller and smaller but are rapidly
being ruined – Marriott‡ would be far happier with soldiers, and
the farm and racehorses are of no interest to him. He is a very
capable man but no man will put his best into something he does
not care about unless he knows that he will lose his job. I do not
want this at all, but I do want the authorities to make it clear that
Racing should be the first and most important thing for his
attention.

The thought that the Stanley House stables might not be full in
1919, and Lambton's complaint that "since the war my income is

★ Mr Jack Joel had given Donoghue £1500 for a second retainer.
† R. J. Colling, son of "Bob" Colling.
‡ Clerk of the Course.

much less and my expenses much bigger", given as his reason for his inability to pay for a Christmas entertainment for his stablemen, gave rise to a correspondence with Lord Derby upon the subject of allowing new owners to come into the stable. Lord Derby had refused to have any of Lord Rosebery's horses at Stanley House, and felt that because of this refusal he could not accept any owned by Giles Loder. This resulted in an embarrassing contretemps with Cicely Lambton, who had evidently told Loder that she would see that at least one of his horses did come into the yard, and had taken it upon herself to write to Lord Derby asking for his agreement to this favour. In his reply he expatiated to her upon the relative positions of master and servant – a lecture which annoyed George Lambton as much as it astounded him. Cicely wrote an apologetic letter to Lord Derby: ". . . what I asked was a personal favour to myself regarding one particular animal. In doing so I treated you as I should have done any friend of George's and my own. I can only say that I am sorry to have made such a mistake . . ."

Lord Derby replied (19 December 1918) to George Lambton:

I am sorry you and Mrs Lambton should both have taken my letter in the way in which you have. It only to my mind emphasises the desirability as I have said that all questions connected with the Stable should be treated as matters of business between you and me. I still have not the least recollection of either having said or written anything to the effect that Giles Loder was a good fellow and that I should like him in the Stable, and I cannot help thinking you are perhaps mixing him up with Decazes. Giles Loder to the best of my knowledge I have never seen in my life nor ever heard of until you wrote to me. I resent your statement that I have lectured Mrs Lambton on the relative positions of master and servant. There is nothing in my letter that would justify you in making such a statement – a statement which I think you will feel on reflection, after 25 years relationship, is unjust and uncalled for. I simply said that you knew that nobody could come into the Stable without previous reference to me and that you had quite rightly made a certain request to me to which I had given a definite answer, and there I thought the matter should have been left, and I still think so. I shall not forget that remark in your letter . . .

George and Cicely spent Christmas at Mells but both were still upset by the Loder incident, and three days later he wrote to Lord Derby:

My dear Eddie

When two friends have a difference of opinion, with resentment on both sides, a correspondence on paper is, I am afraid, apt to increase the difference. I hope in this case that it will not be so – as there is no chance of our meeting I must write.

When I got your letter saying that you could not have Loder in the stable, so far as I was concerned the matter ended. I have placed myself in an unpleasant position but that was my own fault and not yours. This was the business side which has always been maintained by you and me with regard to stable matters – now Cicely's letter to you was essentially not on the business side of our relations. She asked you as a personal favour if you would reconsider the case, and allow this one animal to be trained by me, and that in doing so you would relieve us from an unpleasant position – considering the intimate and friendly terms we are on, I can see nothing wrong in her doing so – it was a simple matter to say "yes or no" – the matter was finished. Your answer if it is not a lecture on the way she should behave as your trainer's wife then I do not understand English, the very fact that you and I have been such friends made me resent it the more, especially as the ten years that I have been married to Cicely has certainly never given you the least reason for thinking that she wants to interfere with the business of the stable in any way. I hate having any trouble with you and have always tried to keep the worries of the stable away from you – I must give you some facts re Giles Loder. In the autumn of 1916 he wrote from France saying that Gilpin was giving up, and that if I could take his horses he would like to send them, that he did not intend having more than six or seven horses in training – this was shortly after you had offered to take a *few* of Rosebery's horses and he had declined that. I wrote to you about Loder but for some reason there was some delay in my answering Loder and curiously enough when I did, our letters crossed, his saying that Gilpin had changed his mind and was going on.

Happily their antagonism was only temporary, and it was not long before Lord Derby was writing: "We are much too old friends to quarrel and I am only sorry that there should have been this difference of opinion between us" (however, Loder's horse did not come to Stanley House).

Nevertheless the outlook for the first post-war season, which was less than two months away, did not seem bright to Lambton. The services of Joe Cannon were thought to be superfluous, and Lamb-

ton's sense of loyalty to his staff was severely tested. He explained
to Lord Derby:

For nearly two years I carried on, not only without Cannon but
with the exception of Osgood nearly all my good men away – so,
although it gives me a lot more work it can be done – but there is
another side which is the disagreeable one; that is having to send
Cannon away after so many years faithful service without any
certainty of his getting a suitable job, and what makes it worse is
the fact that none of his belongings are worth a shilling and I do
not suppose that he has been able to put anything or very little
away himself. I have no knowledge about that, but I do know
that for the last two years with the cost of living, etc. he has had a
hard job to make both ends meet. That is the case with most of us
and with sixpence in the £ income tax and the cost of everything
double, if I had not made money with my yearlings and foals I
should have been on the wrong side, on the bare necessities of life
these past four years.

   If it had not been for the facts re Cannon that I have given you I
should myself have proposed to you that Cannon should go, and
that you should give me a rise, but when it came to doing it I
found it impossible without the feeling that I should all my life be
ashamed of having done so – of course if he could get a place the
difficulty would be solved but there is hardly a trainer who can
even stand a man of their own class in their business. It is foolish,
but it is so – and I am afraid that no one is likely to take him on as a
private trainer.

In the early part of 1919 Lambton suggested that Lord Derby
might like to buy a horse to run in the Grand National. Lord Derby
replied (15 February):

Thanks for your letter about the Grand National horse. I have
telegraphed to you to do nothing further as the price is higher
than I am prepared to go. If this Coal Strike comes off there will
be no Grand National or any other racing either until it is all
settled.
   I saw some of the Stewards of the French Jockey Club today
and they tell me probably racing will begin about the 1st May at
Longchamps. It is to be a sort of joint meeting of the different
Societies and all profit is to go to the wounded soldiers fund.

Lord Derby also made it clear that he thought the important
French races would be easy to win as "they have no horses here at

all", and asked Lambton's advice as to whether he should send three or four of his mares to France: "Decazes says he has room for mares at his stud and he would willingly take any of mine there. He has got a very good Stud Groom and of course anything foaled in France would be eligible to run for French Races."

In April the sudden death of Mr "Fairie" Cox, who had won Classics with Galeottia, Bayardo, Lemberg and My Dear, in addition to his 1917 Triple Crown winner Gay Crusader, caused Lord Derby to ask:

> What is going to happen to poor Cox's horses? Do you think it would be possible to buy Manilardo privately and if so for what price? He is in the Grand Prix and of course in that his nomination is not void. If I could buy him now and get him sent over at once I think he must have a great chance. . . . I do not know if there are many difficulties in getting a horse over but I am sure the War Office people would help us to do it.
>
> To go back to Manilardo I should think a fair price for him would be about £4,000 with a couple of thousand more if he won the Grand Prix.

Manilardo, a full brother to the 1917 Derby winner Gay Crusader, had made a tremendous impression when winning the Wood Ditton Stakes at Newmarket on his début at the Craven meeting, but the death of his owner caused all his future engagements to become null and void.

Whilst Lambton pondered the thought of buying Manilardo, he also had high hopes that Keysoe, by Swynford, might prove a top-class three-year-old, and thought that she would put up a good show in the One Thousand Guineas, particularly as her rivals seemed of little account. She was a light-framed filly lacking in muscle but had pleased him in her work. However she failed to reach a place behind Sir Edward Hulton's Roseway, and the disappointed trainer wrote to her owner: "Keysoe ran a wretched race. Donoghue said that he could hardly hold her for two furlongs, and when he did get her steadied down that she dropped her bit and would not try at all." She did not run in The Oaks, but Lord Derby was home from Paris for a few days and was disappointed that he had no colt good enough to run in The Derby – "I would have liked to have had a runner – it gives one an interest in the race that one would not otherwise have." A week before Epsom he wrote (22 May) to Lambton:

I want you to help a French friend of mine, the Marquis de Saint Sauveur. He will manage for the future any horses I may have in France as I am afraid poor old Dubos although better will never be capable of doing very much in the future.

St Sauveur is going to England today. He is a very good fellow, done extraordinarily well as a Flying man throughout the War. He married a very pretty and nice girl just before the War broke out but unfortunately he suffers from being very poor. He is anxious to start a business here of the same kind as Marcus Beresford's and is being backed up and indeed I think to a certain extent financed by some of the principal racing people in France. He intends to go down to Newmarket on either Saturday or Sunday and will call upon you.

Lord Derby also told Lambton that he did not wish to sell Stedfast,* whom he considered to be Chaucer's best son, giving as an added reason that he had no other horse suitable as a stallion. At the same time he proposed that Lambton should write to him in Paris every Saturday – "It makes it so much more interesting for me out here to know beforehand what is going to run."

Happily Keysoe justified Lambton's high opinion by midsummer and won two races at Goodwood before triumphing in the 1919 St Leger and thus emphasizing the old-time principle "Mate the winner of the St Leger with the winner of The Oaks." This victory delighted everyone at Stanley House, particularly as Keysoe's half-brother Archaic was showing enormous potential as a two-year-old, winning at Goodwood before being placed at the Doncaster St Leger meeting twenty-four hours after Keysoe's Classic success. Lambton wrote to Lord Derby in glowing terms about his future but added:

. . . I do not think Archaic ought to run again this year. He would not beat Tetratema in the Middle Park but he would be quite likely to win the Dewhurst, but it would entail a hard preparation and he is a likely horse for The Derby and the Grand Prix. He is a very late foal. We hear that the strike is over, and the railwaymen say that they have got the best of it. We hope that it is not true, but of course their leaders will attempt to make it so . . . the Unions are trying hard to make the Stablemen strike, but I do not think

---

* Stedfast won twenty races, including the Coronation Cup, the Hardwicke Stakes, and the Jockey Club Stakes, and was second in both the Two Thousand Guineas and The Derby.

they will succeed. I do think now that the winter is coming on that the married men will have to get 45 shillings – with the price of boots and clothes and food . . . they cannot live decently on less.

At Christmas Lord Derby gave every Stanley House stableman a suit and a pair of gloves, and sent Lambton a substantial cheque as a present. Yet trainers were not finding it easy to break level when only charging 70 shillings a week per horse, and Lambton spoke out against those trainers who hoped to make their living from betting and were content to charge lower fees in the hope of being sent horses. Carslake was engaged to ride Archaic and Keysoe the following season whenever he was available, at £1000 and 5 per cent, and young Jack Colling received a £2000 retainer to ride other Stanley House-trained horses.

In the first days of the New Year George Lambton received a letter from Bohemia which saddened him:

Dear Lambton,

Trusting your feelings towards my brother Charles [Kinsky] are the same as his towards you I am fulfilling a sad duty in informing you of his death.

Although having had in 1916 heavy attacks of weakness of the heart he recovered and could subsequently take up his normal life. Since October last these attacks renewed between them, however he was all right again. His last two days were complicated by bronchitis, though he was laid up in bed only 1½ days and passed away very quietly on the 10th December.

I am giving you in short outlines part of his last will in translation:

Remembering George Lambton being always such a good friend to me, perhaps the very best I ever met in all my life, I bequeath to his children John and Anne the sum of 250,000 Kronen each. These sums have to be delivered within 3 months time. I am however afraid the delivery of these sums will take a good while and meet with some difficulties, as the Government is unwilling to allow any amount of money to pass out of the country.

Should this be the case be sure I will watch over the interests of your children as good as possible and in poor Charles' intention. ★

★ The Lambton children never received these legacies.

George Lambton wrote to the *Daily Telegraph* concerning Count Kinsky:

In justice to a very gallant and honourable gentleman I should like to clear his memory from a wicked and baseless slander that was started in the early days of the war . . . The slander was this, that on the outbreak of war Prince Kinsky instructed his groom to poison his hunters in order to prevent them being commandeered by the Government. Now Prince Kinsky and I had hunted together for four years previous to the war. Immediately I heard this story I wrote to his groom who had previously been groom to Lord Annally when Master of the Pytchley Hounds. He telegraphed back "Not one word of truth in the story." He also wrote to me expressing his indignation and surprise that such a slander should have been started, and that for one moment it should have gained credence. I saw Prince Kinsky just before he left for Austria which he did immediately after war was declared on Serbia. He asked me to do all in my power to get his hunters allotted to his friends if they were commandeered by the Government. I am glad to say that four of his old favourites were carrying two generals – both old friends of his . . . it is so easy to start a lie, so difficult to lay it low.

Archaic wintered well, but was unplaced in the Two Thousand Guineas. A fortnight later he was last in the Newmarket Stakes, but Lambton was not despondent and attempted to persuade Donoghue to accept the mount on Archaic in The Derby. Donoghue prevaricated with his customary determination to leave his decision until the eleventh hour. This exasperated Lambton to such an extent that he agreed with Lord Derby that the ride on Archaic should be given to the French jockey Bellhouse after Carslake was claimed by "Atty" Persse for Tetratema.

From Paris Lord Derby had written (20 May 1920):

I'll get St Sauveur to come and see me about Bellhouse. He is a great believer in him. He says he is a very strong and honest jockey and I have therefore told him to see if he could get hold of him and let me know this evening when I shall telegraph to you. He thinks he would no doubt be able to get him and he would be able to cross next week to Newmarket and ride him two or perhaps 3 days at exercise. In addition to which he will try to get him to go over the Monday of Epsom week in order to have a ride at Epsom at exercise on Tuesday morning or perhaps we could possibly give him a mount in some race. I do not know what documents are necessary for Bellhouse to get his riding licence in England but I would ask you to see to this.

Lord Derby promised Bellhouse £500 if he won The Derby on Archaic, and £200 win or lose, but at the last minute Donoghue attempted to have the mount, pleading with George Lambton to let him ride Archaic at Epsom. Feeling that he was placed in an invidious position, Lambton phoned Lord Derby in Paris, and over the telephone it was decided that Bellhouse should have the mount. Lord Derby elaborated his reasons in a letter the next day:

> I could not hear you on the telephone and unfortunately therefore could not talk with you so I am sending you a telegram. I do not think it would be fair to Bellhouse now to take him off Archaic. He is very keen about riding him. He has given up several mounts in order to go and ride him at exercise and although I could make that up to him, still I think it would be looked upon as a tremendous reflection on him, which he would resent and other jockeys here would resent for him, and if they did good-bye to any chance of winning the Grand Prix as they can ride foul more successfully here than any place I have ever seen. I consulted with both Alice and Victoria before I sent the telegram. They both agree with me and moreover they think that you will probably find Bellhouse a very good jockey, strong, reliable and knows how to ride a waiting race. I am very sorry for all these bothers and difficulties and I feel that you would have preferred Donoghue but still I am sure that you will agree with me that under the circumstances the change could not be made at so late an hour.

Towards the middle of May, Archaic gave Keysoe five pounds in a trial gallop and won convincingly. Lambton jubilantly wrote:

> Archaic did enough to make it certain that he is a good horse and quite likely to win The Derby – but his age is against him and he might get upset by the Derby crowd. Will you ask Rosebery if I can saddle in The Durdans. . . . I do not think I shall send Archaic to Epsom until Tuesday, then he will not have to go on the Downs at all, which is a good thing as they are crowded with gypsies . . .

In The Derby Archaic finished second – beaten 2 lengths – to

Major Giles Loder's Spion Kop. It was a fine performance on the part of Archaic, but nevertheless Lambton wrote the next day: "I saw Giles Loder and he told me that he has decided to run Spion Kop in the Grand Prix – I am afraid that his horse will recover from his race quicker than Archaic – for he is not such a big horse and fitter and harder." Such news disappointed Lord Derby, for he thought that Archaic would have a great chance in the Grand Prix as the French horses were useless. However, he told Lambton: "There are two considerations that we must have in mind. First that no permanent harm should come to the horse from running, and secondly that it would be inadvisable to run him unless he is at all events as well as he was on Derby Day, because he is sure to be tremendously backed here. I only wish Spion Kop was not coming over." Archaic did not run, and to everyone's amazement Spion Kop failed to reach the first three.

Despite Donoghue's cavalier behaviour over riding Archaic at Epsom, Lambton was still keen that he should be stable jockey in 1921. Lord Derby offered him a £4000 retainer, telling his trainer:

> Now with regard to Donoghue there was a time when you did not much like Donoghue and did not think he was very straight but apparently there is now no objection to him and personally I should be very pleased to take him on next year but I could not undertake to pay him anything approaching the very high salary that White gave. If he could be got at a reasonable retainer I should be very glad to consider it.

By early autumn George Lambton was contemplating his own future. He told friends that he thought "that the people of England have got into a rotten state – sooner or later I suppose we shall have our own revolution – that is what we are working up for". In a letter to Lord Derby he pointed out: "I have just got to that age when I must think of what is going to happen when I die . . .." He considered whether or not he should purchase Mesnil Warren outright, but believed that it might not be economic from his point of view as the house had been allowed to get into a very bad state of repair externally, and no repainting had been carried out since 1910, although he was under the impression that Lord Derby had authorized various renovations.

He wrote to Lord Derby on 28 June, and received a reply written before his friend went to Evian for three weeks:

> Now with regard to the house. I had thought of the rates, taxes,

etc. when I offered it to you but you remember *under the agreement* when you take over the house as yours *you get £200 a year more.* Of course I do not know how far that would go towards covering the rates and taxes but you would *in addition get all the percentage money* instead of its now being limited to £500 a year, and I should hope that in most years that would mean a considerable addition. *If however you would like it better I would leave the house as mine releasing the sum now invested* and *also the extra percentage over £500* and *giving you the right to buy the house from me at any time that you might wish.* Whichever way you take it I hope it would mean a considerable addition to your salary and it is with that view that I make these proposals. There is of course no hurry for you to decide and you can let me know at any time.

A more immediate problem concerned a possible successor to Joe Cannon, who had rashly and untruthfully told the Jockey Club when applying for a trainer's licence that Lord Derby would send him some horses. George Lambton expressed his ideas:

I am very sorry for the old fellow, but he has no claim on you whatsoever. But in connection with this, I do think it is very bad that old stablemen etc. should have no other home but the work-house. . . . I told you some time ago that I thought I had got the right man for the job – he is a son of Armstrong the trainer. I have had him here for the last ten days, and I like him and he is just what I want. 21 years old, very quiet, steady intelligent boy well educated . . . I have told him that if he comes here his place is to make himself useful to Osgood in every way that he can, but not to interfere with his work in any way – also to make himself thoroughly acquainted with the system of keeping the books, entries etc. . . . he is also to come out in the mornings, as a spare man of that sort is invaluable in a big stable. The running of a big stable is twice the work that it used to be and I think, if you agree, that Armstrong will be a valuable addition to the stable.

Lord Derby did agree, and Gerald Armstrong was taken on at £300 a year.

August found the Stanley House horses running below their true form, and Archaic and Keysoe were two who were smitten by a disease caused by insects. Lambton suggested that the failure of the Derby horses to contest valuable races might cost their owner £12,000, and wrote to his brother Jack asking the Stewards of the Jockey Club to investigate as to whether or not the insects lived in any particular part of the Heath, for Gilpin's stable was equally affected. Lord Derby was about to leave the British Embassy in Paris, and on 8 September he wrote:

It is indeed a gloomy outlook now that we have once got this beastly bug into the Stable. Still we were lucky to win so many races in the last two months and I hope that before the end of the year the horses may come in form again though I am afraid it looks as if Archaic and Keysoe were done for the year.

My resignation is now announced and I shall be home somewhere about the 20th of November for good.

Now about this bug. I talked to a man yesterday who had experience of horse ranches some years ago in America. He tells me he believes that this bug existed at one time there but some cure was found for it. He suggests that I should get from you a proper detailed Veterinary report on the subject and send it, as I can do through my great friend the American Ambassador, to the American Ministry of Agriculture which he says is first rate. They might be able to advise us on the subject.

In further letters (16 and 20 September) he wrote:

There is a rumour here that they have got this beastly heel trouble in the racing stables at Chantilly. Certainly a lot of the horses have got something very much like it and the Pasteur Institute is most anxious to get something on which they could start enquiries. I told them that you had so far not found any insect but if you could get the Vet to get what I think they call a scraping off one of the sore places and put it in an hermetically sealed culture bottle they might be able to discover something . . . about your own affairs please do not think in the least I wanted to hurry you. I know how fearfully busy and anxious you must have been. I was only afraid that you might think that I was not doing anything and as long as you are content I am perfectly ready to arrange the matter whenever you like and whatever we decide can be ante-dated to this date.

Eventually George Lambton agreed to buy Mesnil Warren, with Lord Derby generously allowing him a 4 per cent mortgage on the property.

As planned, Lord Derby returned from Paris at the end of November. His departure from the French capital was regretted by many, for as an English "milord" he had captured great attention in

Paris, and by his personality was instrumental in changing the attitude of France towards Britain. Before he left the Embassy he gave a farewell dinner at which the sixty guests who honoured the occasion included the President of the Republic and Marshall Foch. Commenting upon Lord Derby's ambassadorship, the Paris correspondent of *The Times* wrote: "rank, fortune and knowledge of affairs are solid foundations upon which his success has been built, and that success has been cemented by a shrewd uprightness of character . . ."

After his return, Lord Derby began contemplating the future of his racing interests from a financial viewpoint, and told George Lambton that he thought it unprofitable to have horses belonging to other owners in the Stanley House stables.

> My own idea is that what I receive only just about pays their actual expenses, and therefore nothing is contributed towards the salaries or for the rent, rates and taxes which all fall on me. If that is the case I should either have to put up the amount I ask from the other people very considerably which I should not like doing or else revert to being a stable simply for my own horses which I do not suppose you would much object to. . . . I ask you not to show this letter nor to speak of this letter to anyone. Can you give me any idea of what difference it would make to me from a financial point of view if I decided to ask you to become, as you were for my father, my private trainer and have nobody else in the stable?

The newspapers learned of the possibility of Lambton becoming Lord Derby's private trainer, and before leaving for Biarritz Lord Derby commented: "It amused me very much and I wondered if it would not be a good thing to make use of the statement to get rid of Mrs Arthur James, who I cannot stand and who I know worries you . . ." Fifty-three-year-old Mrs Arthur James, who had been a personal friend of King Edward VII, was one of the few women owners on the Turf. When her husband, a member of the Jockey Club, died in 1917, she elected to continue the Coton House Stud, which she inherited from him.

In January 1921 Steve Donoghue went to the office of the Newmarket solicitors Rustom and Lloyds and signed his part of the agreement to ride for Lord Derby, who admitted to Lambton: "There is something that I want you to do for me. It is a bit of a superstition. Twice over when the list of Horses in Training has been printed in the *Sporting Chronicle*, and my horses have been

mixed up with the horses of other people in the Stable we have had
bad luck. Please see that mine are listed separately." A month later
George and Cicely Lambton took a holiday at Menton, where they
rented a villa. They missed seeing Lord Derby in the South of
France by a day, for he returned to England twenty-four hours
before they arrived.

On his return, Lambton, ever thoughtful of others, told Lord
Derby in a letter:

> There is a thing in connection with Racing that wants looking
> into. There is no sort of Fund for the relief of old stablemen,
> jockeys, etc., except the Bentinck Fund: that is very badly off and
> the most a man gets is £15 a year which is not enough to keep him
> out of the work house. I do not suppose that there is another
> business in the world where the worn-out servants are so badly
> looked after. I think that with the money that there is in Racing,
> that some scheme might be started, in which trainers, owners,
> *jockeys* and stablemen should have to help to make a Fund – and
> you are the man to start it.

In March 1921 the traditional house party held at Knowsley for
the Grand National meeting was revived after a lapse of seven years.
The King and Queen were guests of honour, with the Prince of
Wales, Lord and Lady Pembroke, Lord Marcus Beresford, the
Marquis and Marquise de Saint Sauveur and George and Cicely
Lambton amongst the other guests in the party. To entertain them
after dinner one evening Lord Derby enterprisingly arranged for
the world light-heavyweight boxing champion, Georges Carpentier, to give a display. The French press were delighted at the news
of this exhibition bout, but unfortunately Carpentier drew blood
from his sparring partner, who was somewhat intoxicated and
who, to make matters worse, was heard to belch as he staggered
drunkenly around the ring. An embarrassed Carpentier was worried that the Queen would be horrified at the sight of blood, but in
reality his worries were groundless. Slightly more worrying for
Lord Derby was another occasion when he engaged George Robey
to entertain the royal party. Whilst a fellow-comedian was on stage,
Robey sat next to the King and persisted in saying "that was a good
one, George" whenever the comedian cracked a joke.

Whilst the Grand National meeting was taking place, ominous
clouds were gathering over the coalmining industry, due to the
desire of employers to reduce wages, and the determination of the
miners to resist such reductions. On 1 April a coal strike com-

menced, which the miners called a "lock-out". For some days it seemed probable that the railway workers and the transport vehicle workers would join them. Lord Derby was perturbed by the political scene, and commented:

> Things look a little better but we are by no means out of the wood and personally I cannot see the way out of the impasse. It is a question of principle and it is very difficult for either side to give way. Anyhow I am perfectly certain negotiations will be very protracted. They may agree on some general scheme but it will have to be worked out in detail before I believe the men will return to work, and though I think it is as well to go on with the horses as if racing would take place, I myself do not believe there will be any racing for the next three weeks. But this may be a somewhat pessimistic view to take . . .

In fact there was no racing in England between 2 April and 29 April, and it was even suggested in some quarters that the government deliberately insisted on the cancellation of race meetings in their efforts to deprive the striking miners of their daily excitement of "studying form".

About this time His Highness the Aga Khan was dining at Mrs Edwin Montagu's* house and found himself sitting next to Mrs Raymond Asquith. In the course of conversation she vehemently urged him to consider racing in England and suggested that her brother-in-law should buy a few mares and yearlings on his behalf. The next morning His Highness wrote to George Lambton from the Ritz Hotel asking him to call to discuss the project. Lambton agreed to the commission to buy bloodstock, but declined the Aga's invitation to become his private trainer. However in the course of the next two years he bought Mumtaz Mahal, Cos and Teresina for the Aga Khan, who subsequently claimed that he had wanted to buy the yearling colt by Tracery out of Miss Matty to whom the name Papyrus was given, but that Lambton had declined to bid as he thought the colt too small and on the stocky side. Whether or not the claim was correct, the fact remains that Papyrus won the 1923 Derby.

---

* In 1915 Venetia Stanley, a daughter of Baron Sheffield, had married Edwin Montagu, second son of Lord Swaythling. Venetia was one of a coterie who included the Asquiths, the Horners, the Grenfells, Lady Diana Manners, Patrick Shaw-Stewart and Charles Lister, son of Lord Ribblesdale. All the men in this coterie were Etonians.

In mid-April 1921 Lord Derby told George Lambton:

I still take a pessimistic view and I do not think there is the least chance of any racing for 3 weeks or a month. The miners meet on Friday. My own view is that there may be a split between them and some may go back but I do not think they will go back in Scotland, Lancashire or South Wales and until they do the strike cannot be called off. Meanwhile there will have to be discussions between owners and men which will take at least a fortnight if not longer and I very much doubt our having either the Newmarket Meetings, Chester or the Jubilee. I only hope I may be wrong, but between ourselves I saw Lloyd George yesterday and I make this forecast on what he told me. He knew nothing about racing being stopped but of course it is not extraordinary he should not do so, but I know he will do his best to secure resumption as soon as possible.

I have just got the racing accounts for 1920 and I find that notwithstanding all the Stud fees there was a loss on racing of £12,000. I shall have to go into the accounts with you as of course I cannot afford to go on like that, and I shall have to think to cut down the number of horses I have got. There is one thing however that I do not understand and that is repairs at Newmarket coming to £4,700. It seems to me perfectly gigantic.

Once racing was resumed Lambton was delighted by the Manchester Cup victory of March Along – who had virtually been trained for the final week before the race by Cicely, as George had influenza – but he was not optimistic that the Stanley House horses held more than outside chances for Classics, although he thought that Glorioso "might have something to say in The Derby". He himself had something to say when he heard that Lord Derby proposed to buy a new horse-box, and suggested: "I should think that for places like Ascot these vans might be a tremendous advantage." At the back of Lord Derby's mind was the thought that a motorized horse-box would be available to transport his horses in times of rail strikes. He wrote to Lambton:

I have seen the Leyland people who live in my part of the world and I know would go out of their way to make a good job for me, and they tell me they bought back a lot of the lorries that they supplied to the Government and which had practically not been used. They guarantee to put them into thorough order and tell me that one could look upon them as giving at least 10 years work. The whole question however is would you use the motor except in such abnormal times as this.

Meanwhile, Lambton was trying desperately to train Glorioso, a colt by Swynford, for The Derby, but had to admit:

Glorioso did not put much heart into his work, and he does not like to stretch himself out on firm going . . . . "Vandy" Beatty has been to Epsom, he says that although the course is in good order it is as hard as the road and like glass round Tattenham Corner – all sign of rain seems to have gone. Beatty says that nothing but 48 hours' rain will have any affect upon the Epsom course . . . I want Glorioso to avoid Epsom; at the best with good going it was only a forlorn hope . . . Lady Alice will tell you about the horse-box – I went in it yesterday and do not like it much – and expect the body can be greatly improved – I believe it to be the first horse-box Leyland has built.

Motor cars were a pet abomination of George Lambton, partly because he was not mechanically minded and never learned to drive a car with authority. Years earlier he had rebuked Danny Maher for arriving on the Newmarket gallops in his newly acquired motor car – "Danny, you can have your car or you can have your horses, but you have got to choose. You are a paid servant, as I am, along with all the other boys in the stable." But, as Lambton had told Lord Derby: "I have no experience of motor vans . . . I hear that people are buying them where they can, but I should say that you would be much safer to deal with a firm you know . . . if you get a horse-box I hope that they will get it done by Epsom."

By mid-May Lambton was ill, and he went to Cromer on the Norfolk coast – "it has done me a lot of good, and there is nothing the matter now, except that I feel so damnably weak . . . I have been looking at the other Derby horses – none seem to have much chance."

On the Monday before Epsom Lambton wrote:

There was a complete change in the weather at 4.30 am this morning. Fortunately I was awake, so I got up and managed to get Glorioso away in the special which left at 6.00 am. A tremendous crowd of horses for one special – over 70 I believe. Last night I released Donoghue – I do not know if he has made any arrangements, but if he has, I see in the papers that Carslake has not got a mount in The Derby – if that is so he is the man for Glorioso.

Donoghue had behaved with total lack of loyalty in squirming out of his commitment to ride Glorioso, but from his point of view his disloyalty paid dividends, for he rode Humorist to victory whilst the 66–1 Glorioso was a forlorn failure.

Six weeks after The Derby, Lady Randolph Churchill, mother of Winston, died following a fall at Mells, where she was a guest of the Horners. She slipped on the staircase and badly fractured her leg near the ankle. She was taken back to her London home; gangrene set in, the leg was amputated and she died on 29 June. Within the year (1921) Lord Derby's mother died at the age of eighty-one. Fourteen years earlier and within months of her husband's death, she had written letters to her children which were not to be opened until after her death. In her letter to her son she wrote: "My darling Eddie . . . you have been the best and dearest of sons to me . . ."

Lord Derby was still anxious to have runners in France, and suggested that some of his horses should be entered for the Deauville races. However he was not amused by an editorial in the *Winning Post* written by Bob Sievier, whom George Lambton detested, which stated:

> Having spent the Grande Semaine in Paris it has been impressed upon us more than ever that the British still remain "perfidious Albion" in the vacillating spirit of the French nation . . . in brief France has returned to her pre-war muttons or more appropriately her potage. It is only natural that our late Ambassador in France, Lord Derby, does not come in contact with the people, and is not thrown into that everyday life, only upon which a serious opinion can be formulated. This also applies to his Lordship's dashing trainer, the Hon. George Lambton, whose brief excursions to Paris give him but a "microbic" opportunity of gleaning the stubborn truth – otherwise doubtless he would have addressed himself to a sporting daily paper long, long ago.

However, there may have been some truth in Sievier's editorial, for on the day of the Grand Prix – won by Lemonora – Lord Derby ran March Along in the Prix d'Ispahan. A patriotic English eye-witness wrote after the race: "Lord Derby's colt was boxed in, and Donoghue had no more chance of extricating himself than is given to a convict to escape from Dartmoor. Indeed it was less, for the convict has a kind of sporting chance and has been known to avail himself of it, but Donoghue was never even given a hopeless one. In a fair and sporting contest March Along would have won."

At the end of August Lord Derby was staying at Grey Walls, a house at Gullane on the Firth of Forth that he rented every year. He wrote to Lambton: "I am a little disturbed at having no good two year olds and we must have a talk about the mares. I wonder whether we had not better get rid of a good many of them and buy some other blood to go with the Swynford." Understandably Lord Derby was also disturbed and never totally happy with Donoghue's high-handed interpretation of his retainers, and told Lambton:

> Now the following is something which I have written for you to read to Donoghue if you think fit. . . . Donoghue receives a retainer from me. Nobody else in the stable contributes to it, and therefore even if my horse may not seem to have the same chance as a horse belonging to somebody else in the stable, it is my horse he must ride, and I must insist on this being rigidly adhered to in the future.
>
> I spoke to Donoghue at Deauville, and said I hoped he would ride for me again next year. He said he would be ready to do so but there were certain alterations he would like to make in the agreement. . . . There is one other condition which I think I must impose and that is that he shall only ride abroad in France on Sundays after having received written permission from me. It is quite impossible for any jockey to be at his best, if after riding in England on Saturday he flies to France, rides in France on Sunday, and flies back again.

Before the end of 1921, when George Lambton was elected people's warden at St Agnes' Church, Lord Derby was again financially worried by the cost of his racing, and claimed:

> It is quite impossible for me not to sell some horses that will fetch at all events a fairly good price in view of the fact of the general expenses of racing. There was a loss last year, and from what I can make out there will be a bigger loss this year. I do not consider this to be anybody's fault, for I know that it is not – very far from it – but the fact remains that unless I can, at the December sales, get a certain sum of money from animals I sell, racing would cost me more than I can afford . . .

Nevertheless, his generosity towards others caused him to give 5 per cent of his gross racing winnings each season from 1921 onwards to the benevolent department of the British Legion, of which he was a Vice-President.

Lord Derby also told Lambton:

I am sorry to say Horace* has had a tremendous row with the whole lot of us, about a joint present to Princess Mary.† It is too long a story to write about, but his anger is now centred on me. He has been making awful scenes also about his office. Jack‡ went with me to see him yesterday, and I think he would confirm what I say, that there is no doubt he has got signs of softening of the brain. He cannot remember anything and he gets in the most violent fits of passion. He was most awfully rude to me personally, and apparently bears great resentment towards me as he will put into my mouth things which I certainly never said.

I am so sorry to hear of poor Lady Anne's§ illness. I hope she is going on all right. I know Jack is very anxious. I have just called there and the bulletin, which probably you have heard, is not very reassuring. It says she has got congestion of the lungs complicated with pleurisy. Her strength is fairly well maintained considering the severity of the attack. I am afraid it will put her back a great deal.

By February Lord Derby had returned to Knowsley from the South of France. On the 7th he wrote to Lambton:

I am glad you are feeling better and only hope that the weather will be kinder to you than it was to us. Got back here to find very cold weather and tremendous gloom over everybody. Quite apart from political events the fact that this foot and mouth disease has spread so much that all hunting is stopped today, has had a most depressing effect. I saw the Minister of Agriculture yesterday. The outbreak is very bad and I am afraid that they have got no more money left to pay compensation and therefore they will have to let it run its course and not slaughter animals, which is what I believe they do in Germany. Still that would mean that the disease is sure to go on and there probably will be no more hunting this year.

I saw Waldorf Astor at Horace's party last night. He tells me that their animals have had a very bad go of influenza and he really does not know what the consequences will be.

---

* Sir Horace Farquhar, a former Master of the Household to King Edward VII.
† On her engagement to Viscount Lascelles.
‡ His brother, the Earl of Durham.
§ The Earl of Durham's wife.

In May he wrote:

> Did you see that Frisky* won the French One Thousand. She is
> very small but a beautiful little filly, and I should think has got a
> good chance of winning the French Oaks, as there is nothing in it
> that she has not already beaten, and has even got an outside
> chance for the Grand Prix. The race on Sunday was much more
> valuable than appears in the paper as it was 110,000 francs, and
> although that is not much at the present rate of exchange still for
> paying expenses in France the franc is almost at pre-war value.

1922 did not prove a successful year for Lord Derby until the
autumn. There was racing at Liverpool during the days before the
general election which overthrew Lloyd George, and wherever
Lord Derby went he was asked for tips. The first two that he gave
failed to win, but on Thursday 9 November he suggested that
Burnt Sienna and Highbrow would win in his colours. They duly
obliged at lucrative odds, and the following afternoon Selene won
the Liverpool Autumn Cup to make the legion of Derby supporters
happy.

After Selene's victories at Liverpool and at Hurst Park ten days
later a racing correspondent wrote: "As for Selene I do not think
that we have seen her equal, as a small filly, since Wheel of Fortune.
In conformation Selene is as near perfection as you can ever expect.
Her depth and forehand are specially remarkable, and with it all
there is perfect symmetry, length and balance." Lord Derby was
adamant about Selene's future and told Lambton: "Now about
Selene. I quite see the temptation to keep her in training but I have
definitely decided not only is she to go out of training but that she is
to be covered next year as I disagree with Walter's proposal to give
her a rest of a year. I think it is absolutely unnecessary."

Sixty-eight-year-old Walter Alston had been Lord Derby's stud
manager since 1908. Previously he had been with Mr Douglas
Baird, and was acknowledged as being one of the greatest authorities in the kingdom upon bloodstock breeding. Perhaps his greatest
flash of genius was when he bought the ex-selling plater Gondolette, the dam of Sansovino and the grandam of Tranquil and
Selene who in turn became the dam of Derby winner Hyperion. He
outlined the basis of his personal convictions when he wrote:
"There are few things of which one can be sure in breeding but I
think that there is one. If you can afford it and can find the horse,

---

* Owned by Lord Derby.

you should not go to plodders for staying or to pure sprinters for speed, but get both from the same sire – say St Simon to whom all courses were alike.'' He also believed that the only rule was that there were no rules concerning breeding, although he advised Lord Derby that matings should not necessarily be discarded if the first progeny lacked racecourse ability. He often suggested that the same mating should be repeated year after year, with considerable success. Lord Derby once remarked that if his wife, George Lambton and Walter Alston agreed on a yearling he would buy it regardless of cost – but luckily for him they never agreed.

The two-year-old Pharos was also high in the esteem of the public, for Lord Derby's bay colt by Phalaris out of Scapa Flow had won six of the nine races in which he had taken part, and had done much to enable Lord Derby to be second on the list of Winning Owners for the Season.

Before Christmas, George Lambton was asked by Lord Derby if a stranger could come to Mesnil Warren to study his training methods. He wrote back:

What an extraordinary proposal on the part of W. White [an American owner]; I am always delighted to show strangers the horses, either in the stables or at work and do anything I can for them, but to have a total stranger coming out continually in the morning and following me about ''FOR SEVERAL WEEKS'' is really quite out of the question as far as I am concerned. I have often been asked by friends and other people to take their sons or relations as apprentices in the training line, and at my own terms, and I have always refused – and that a man should suggest what White does beats me altogether. No one but an American would have the assurance and the cheek to do it.

George Lambton had been ill during October and November, and early in December had a fall out hunting. Lord Derby commiserated:

I'm afraid it will interfere with your hunting for some time – what an awful bore for you – I am sorry to hear about your eyes. Why do you not recuperate in the South of France. I always think that warm weather has a greater effect on you than anyone else I know . . .

Lord Derby generously offered to pay for the holiday, and at first

Lambton accepted the offer. However he changed his mind and told Lord Derby:

> I hunted again on Friday and Saturday, also on Monday and I got on so well and feel so much better that I do not like the idea of going abroad, and I really think that I am able to hunt as I am now, and it does me more good physically and mentally than anything else. When you proposed my trip I was quite overcome by your kindness; and not feeling very grand at the time I jumped at it. But now I hope you won't think me very ungrateful if I stop in England.

7

At Long Last

In the final days of October 1922, Lloyd George's coalition government had resigned, with *The Times* declaring that the event marked the end of a political epoch. Bonar Law formed a Conservative government with Lord Derby as Secretary for War and the Duke of Devonshire as Colonial Secretary, but his administration was only to last six months before he was compelled to resign on the grounds of ill health.

For the 1923 season Lord Derby had thirty-one horses in training with George Lambton, who also trained fourteen horses for Lord Stanley, Lord Wolverton, Lord d'Abernon, Lord Durham and Mrs Arthur James with Lord Derby's consent. By the spring Pharos was thought to have a brilliant year ahead of him. Sadly he failed in his first race at Pontefract. Lord Derby commented: "It is a great disappointment about Pharos, but I still hope that he will get a mile on the top of the ground. It does look, however, as though the Phalaris's will not stay, and we shall have to consider very carefully next year what mares we mate with him."

However the three-year-old filly Tranquil, by Swynford, was pleasing Lambton in her work and he told Lord Derby "she did well enough for a big mare early in the year to be a very good one later". Starting favourite on her season's début at Newbury, she defeated twenty rival fillies with ease and Lord Derby, mightily pleased, wrote on 16 April:

I was delighted about Tranquil but I am afraid from what you say it will take her all her time to beat Cos in the 1,000. I was also very pleased about Spithead* though I confess to a certain sense of annoyance in view of the fact that you had never even told me he was going to run. So much did I think that he was not going to run when somebody at the War Office asked me in the morning if

* Spithead had won the Thatcham Long Distance Handicap the next afternoon at 100–7.

he had got a chance I said I was sure the announcement of his arrival at Newbury was inaccurate. I quite understand that you may not at times be able to decide until the last moment whether you run or not but if ever there is any change in the programme you send me at the beginning of the week I want you or Murland to send me a telegram. I shall be able to go racing very little indeed and so I am afraid there is not much chance of seeing you as one does at the races and I must therefore depend upon your letters and telegrams for information . . . I had hoped to get down on Tuesday but there is an Army Bill in the House of Lords which I must take . . . I am trying to keep the 1000 guineas day free, but it is very difficult to say that I shall be able to do so, as what with Committees and House of Lords work and one's own work, one never seems to get away at all.

Despite Lord Derby's lack of optimism Tranquil, ridden by E. Gardner,* defeated the Aga Khan's Cos in the One Thousand Guineas by 1½ lengths, yet he was not satisfied with Gardner's ability and was furious that his jockey "threw away" the Manchester Cup on Silurian three weeks later. Lambton admitted that he shared the displeasure and had misgivings about Gardner's future as stable jockey. Lord Derby openly confessed: "I am very perturbed by what you told me about Gardner's riding – it gives me fearful qualms about The Derby – although perhaps a talking to by you may help matters – as I do not think it would be possible to take him off Pharos." He added: "I dislike that boy Beary very much. I am certain he is a wrong'un too. However I will be on the look out for him whenever I am Steward . . ."

Gardner on Pharos finished second to Donoghue on Papyrus in the Derby. Many spectators considered that he rode an injudicious race, and George Lambton was furious when he learned that Gardner had been seen dancing until a late hour on the eve of the race. Forty-eight hours later Gardner failed to finish in the first three on Tranquil in The Oaks – for which she started an even-money favourite – but to be fair to him Tranquil had temporarily trained off. However matters came to a head the week after The Derby, when Silurian won at Kempton ridden by twenty-year-old Tommy Weston, the son of a wagon driver on the Lancashire and Yorkshire railway, who had made a favourable impression upon George Lambton during the past three seasons. Lord Derby appreciated that Gardner's ability and judgement lacked the high standard that he required and wrote to Lambton:

* Whose father was a bookmaker.

I do not like to turn a jockey down after a race such as The Oaks because it really would mean that he would get no further riding. At the same time I think we ought to harden our hearts and in cases such as Silurian in the Ascot Gold Cup put up Weston, telling Gardner perfectly frankly that in certain cases and on certain courses we think horses go better with Weston than they do with him.

Nevertheless by the end of June Lord Derby had written to Gardner terminating his connection as first jockey at Stanley House. He wrote again after receiving a plea from Gardner: "You ask whether my decision is final. It is to this extent that while Mr Lambton has full power to put up any other jockey that he may wish on any of my horses, he has at the same time liberty if he so wishes to employ you from time to time." On Gardner's dismissal Tommy Weston was retained in his stead, and left Middleham to live at Newmarket, where initially he found that there was much heart-burning amongst other Newmarket-based jockeys that a "north country boy" had been given the coveted plum job of first jockey at Stanley House.

Before the summer was over there were rumours that Lord Derby might become a "stop-gap" Prime Minister. Bonar Law had resigned in May, and six months later was dead, stricken by cancer. Curzon seemed his logical successor, although Derby's name was also mentioned, but King George V decided to send for the comparative "outsider" Stanley Baldwin. Within the next eighteen months it seemed once again that Lord Derby might achieve the leadership of the Tory party and ultimately become Prime Minister, but by that time he had lost the ambition necessary to promote his cause, and the opportunity never returned.

Whilst Lord Derby was in the throes of the political upheaval caused by Bonar Law's resignation, George Lambton was again unwell and went to Harrogate to recuperate. Lord Derby spent the later part of August and the first weeks of September at Gullane, and wrote to Lambton telling him how worried he was to hear that Tranquil might not stand up to her St Leger preparation. He added his personal opinion that the connections of The Derby hero, Papyrus, were mad to accept the challenge to race in America, "unless of course they want to sell the horse, and if he won there no doubt they would get a very big price . . ."

On the final day of June 1923 Lord Derby's two-year-old Sansovino (Swynford-Gondolette) made a winning début at Goodwood, and a month later won the historic Gimcrack Stakes at York on the same afternoon that Phaon won a maiden race in his colours. He wrote delightedly:

> Many congratulations on our two wins yesterday. It was most satisfactory, and Sansovino looks as if he might turn out to be quite a good horse. You always thought he might . . . Poor old Horace.★ It is very sad, his death, and yet one is really glad the end came as soon as it did. I went to see him last week, and it really was very distressing, and although he quite knew me, one felt that he was failing very fast, and that one said goodbye to him for the last time. I shall go up for the funeral, and I know you will want to do the same, but I do hope you will think twice before you do it. Everybody will know that you want to go, but that you are going through a cure, and nothing is worse, in such a short cure, than breaking it for one day.

In the weeks before the St Leger, Lambton sent Tranquil to Charles Morton at Wantage for her final preparation, since the filly was heartily sick of the Newmarket gallops. This unusual course of action proved successful. Lord Derby was not at Doncaster to see Tranquil win the St Leger – "I wish I had been at Doncaster, but I am afraid I am getting very lazy about travelling, and once I get settled in a place I like remaining there, but I am very glad that Edward was there to lead her in. I got a letter from 'Portia' in which she says he is still in such a state of excitement he is barely coherent." Lord Derby contemplated how to give a present to Morton: "The only question is, being private trainer to Joel, whether I ought to give him a money present, or whether it would be better to expend the money on a cup and perhaps also a picture of Tranquil." Frustratingly the Stanley House horses started to cough soon after the St Leger meeting and the remainder of the season proved disappointing. However Lord Derby sent a gracious letter to George Lambton at the end of the season:

> Now the end of the racing season has come I must write you one line to thank you most sincerely and most gratefully for all that you have done for me this year, and I am afraid a great deal at the expense of your own health.
>
> It is entirely due to you and your care that I am the head of the winning owners and in the various racing statistics published today there is only one blot and that is that you are not head of the winning trainers.

★ Lord Farquhar.

To be head of the winning owners and breeders; to have the race horse of the year which has won more money than any other; to have the winning stallion;* and to have all four stallions within the first 20 is a record which I should think had never been equalled and certainly never beaten, and it is to you that all this is due.

What is perhaps even more wonderful is looking back over the 30 years for which you have trained for me – because you trained for me before you began for my father. During that time from very small beginnings you have helped us to build up a Stud to which no other in the world is equal, and to keep up an average of winning each year which cannot be compared with. . . .

For all this as I say I am deeply grateful and nobody shares in that gratitude more than Edward, who I am glad to say is as keen, or even keener about racing than I am. . . .

We are in the thick of hard fighting here and with two sons, a son-in-law and a brother fighting Lancashire seats you can imagine I have my hands full, but I do not mean to let anything turn me, if I can help it, from going abroad on December 28th and I count on you to come with us. I have got your place on the train and room at the hotel. I presume you are not bringing a servant. I can arrange for either my servant or Arty's to valet you. I shall try and come down to the Sales but whichever way this Election goes it may be difficult for me to get away. Still I might be able to snatch the afternoon when our animals are sold.

As a result of the final weeks of Tranquil's St Leger preparation under the care of Morton at Wantage, Lord Derby gave much consideration to the possibility of acquiring a training establishment far from Newmarket as a second string to his bow. He mentioned his ideas to George Lambton, told him to make discreet enquiries, and added that he had heard that a Lambourn stables was for sale.

With regard to the Berkshire establishment I do not expect it will be sold this week and the question which we might discuss is whether we should lease it, putting somebody in charge and then be able to send down any horses when the going at Newmarket is too bad or if Marriott puts on too many restrictions. I do not suppose the rent would be very high nor would be the upkeep

---

* Swynford.

and it might pay us hand over fist to have some place where we could send horses so as to do all their initial training when the going is hard at Newmarket leaving them to come back to you for the final winding up.

I expect you have got somebody whom you could put there who would carry out your instructions.

He was disappointed that Tranquil was beaten in the Jockey Club Cup in October – particularly as she had started at odds-on – and confirmed his approval of George Lambton's suggestion that she should be covered in March and then trained for the Ascot Gold Cup, to be taken out of training immediately after the race, win or lose. He knew that Walter Alston would be horrified at the idea, but thought that he as owner and Lambton as trainer might overrule their stud manager.

Throughout 1923 George Lambton had been preparing his Racing Reminiscences which were serialized every Sunday in the *Weekly Dispatch*. The newspaper proudly and justly claimed: "Mr George Lambton's Reminiscences take instant grip of the imagination and the mind. He holds a mirror, crystal clear, to the social and sporting life of a period full of great and romantic happenings. He reflects the manners and the moods, the doings and sayings of men and women who made contemporary history." George Lambton enjoyed writing his memoirs but initially it had been his wife Cicely who encouraged him to put them on paper and insisted that the general public would enjoy reading them.

In October *Men and Horses I Have Known* was published by Thornton Butterworth, price one guinea. The reviews were laudatory, and his wonderful knack of compression was praised: "Not a word is wasted," claimed the *Sunday Sportsman*. "Every sentence carries a Dempsey-like punch. It is a marvellous autobiography, and in its pages we meet every Turf celebrity of the past thirty odd years." George Lambton did not dedicate the book to Cicely in the Preface, but in a subsequent chapter wrote:

I remember once long ago some trainer being discussed and making the remark, "Oh you can wipe him out, he has just been married." I was much chaffed by my friends when at a future date I had cause to alter this opinion and was married myself. I found that by so doing the rough passages of life were made smooth and the pleasant ones delightful. Certainly without the help of my wife this book whether for good or bad would never have seen the light, and it is to her that I dedicate its pages.

In February 1924 George Lambton went to Cap d'Ail: "I am sound again but it has pulled me down a bit – I go into Cannes occasionally and that doctor there has done me a lot of good. Weather delicious. Tommy Weston is at Monte – appears to be leading a very quiet life and a simple one." By March Lambton had returned to Newmarket in the best of spirits, and wrote a paper attacking Marriott, not for the management of the training grounds, but for the rigid rules that he enforced, and his refusal to make any alterations or to try to adapt himself to the special needs of the moment. Lord Derby supported his trainer against Marriott, and confirmed his support:

> I am quite ready to take action about Marriott. I had as a matter of fact a little talk with Hugh Lonsdale at the last meeting and I told him that I was very dissatisfied with the way Marriott was managing things and I should probably write officially to the Stewards to ask them to go into the matter. I told him that I had probably got the largest stable at Newmarket. I paid very highly for the privilege of training on the Heath only to find that one's trainer was thwarted in every way by a man who knows and cares nothing about racing. He was very sympathetic and I think the time has come when I can write to him. It might be better to put it off till after Ascot as we should look rather foolish if we complained that there was no training ground and then perhaps Sansovino won The Derby and we won races at Ascot afterwards.

Lord Derby's comment "I told him that I had probably got the largest stable at Newmarket" was something of an understatement, for his position as one of the mainstays of breeding and racing in Britain was acknowledged by all. His success on the Turf was giving him an exalted position in the Winning Owners List every season, whilst his stallions Chaucer, Swynford, Stedfast and Phalaris were consistently producing winners. In 1923 Swynford, with the winners of thirty races to his credit, headed the List of Winning Stallions.

In his letter, Lord Derby had mentioned the chance that "perhaps" Sansovino might win The Derby in a phrase indicating that he had little more than hope that so glorious an achievement might materialize. However, George Lambton had fancied Sansovino for many weeks, even though the colt was never one of his favourites, as he thought he lacked "guts" and had to be given his own way. It was for that reason that he had worked Sansovino with moderate horses who had to allow him weight, in order to give him confidence and build up his courage. Yet when he was given one searching gallop across the Flat against Pharos and Tranquil, Sansovino came out with flying colours, and made Lambton realize that his chance at Epsom was second to none. Consequently he backed the colt far more heavily than he usually did when he thought a Stanley House horse had an outstanding chance. His one worry was the state of the going – Sansovino needed some give in the ground. Luckily the rain commenced the weekend before Epsom and the torrential downpour continued unabated for days, with some parts of England soaked by as much as four inches within thirty-six hours. On the eve of The Derby George Lambton's confidence increased still further as a result of saddling the three-year-old Dunmow to win the final race. Dunmow won easily, and Lambton knew that Sansovino could give him the best part of two stone!

Derby Day, 4 June 1924, dawned wet and cold, with conditions at Epsom reminiscent of the mud at Passchendaele. Few ventured to the paddock to inspect the heavily rugged runners prior to the race – but those who did so thought that Sansovino looked trained to the minute. Because of the rain he became the most heavily backed horse for the race and started favourite at 9–2. Lord Derby's colt took up the running as the field rounded Tattenham Corner and won by six lengths – the first winning favourite since Sunstar in 1911. He had turned the race into a procession. "Lord Derby wins!" the rain-soaked crowd was shouting long before Tommy Weston and Sansovino had reached the winning post, and pandemonium broke loose as a jubilant Lord Derby walked out onto the course to lead in his hero, who was surrounded by mounted police. "At last, at long last," muttered members of the Jockey Club as they congratulated the beaming almost overwhelmed winning owner who was shaking hands with all and sundry oblivious of the rain. It had been a memorable day in Turf history: a colt owned by an Earl of Derby had won the "Blue Riband" for the first time in 137 years.

Lord Derby's first words to George Lambton were: "I am so glad for your sake." Twenty miles away at Eton Nancy Lambton, accompanied by her old nanny, had spent the day with John. When they heard the news of Sansovino's triumph they rushed into the High Street, where they did a war dance of jubilation, whilst at Mesnil Warren, Teddy and the butler put up Union Jacks and other flags.

On the way to the start of The Derby, Tommy Weston's white scarf had become caught up in a buttonhole of his black silk jacket, giving the impression of a white button. Superstitiously believing that this was an omen of good fortune, Lord Derby decreed that in

future his racing colours should contain one white button on the
jacket.

In the evening the Queen and the Duchess of York dined with
Lady Derby at Derby House and the King gave his traditional
dinner at Buckingham Palace to the Jockey Club. On the reverse
side of his menu, Lord Wavertree pompously wrote, "Dinner to
members of the Jockey Club on the occasion of Lord Derby
winning The Derby with Sansovino by Swynford out of Gondolette, sold to him by Lord Wavertree for that purpose."

In retrospect Peter Purcell Gilpin, doyen of trainers, wrote:

Sansovino bore eloquent tribute to the skill of his trainer, Mr
Lambton. Clean, hard and fighting fit for the ordeal before him,
he was a picture of the trainer's art, and there was not a soul that
knew him but was delighted to congratulate Mr Lambton on the
attainment of every trainer's ambition.

Another comment, also written concerning The Derby result,
stated:

Mr Lambton has aged a bit in the last year or so – and his clever
wife gets younger looking on the other hand – and the strain of
the last few weeks must have told severely . . . I am sure that the
indefatigable Lord Durham and his twin brother, and the more
imposing Admiral of the Fleet Sir Hedworth Meux (who is far
less like the Lambtons in looks) felt very proud of George.
Sansovino's trainer is undoubtedly the most interesting looking
of the family.

With some of his winnings over Sansovino George Lambton
commissioned Sir Edwin Lutyens to make additions to Mesnil
Warren, where the staff included a butler, a footman, a nanny and a
cook who loved backing horses. When they won the food was
excellently cooked; when the horses failed, the cooking became
abysmal. George Lambton always insisted that the household was
run with the utmost efficiency, and demanded total punctuality
from his children, explaining that it was as easy to be on time as to
be late. He also demanded tidiness, although he never considered
that the demand applied to himself and would throw his clothes
indiscriminately over the bedroom floor, expecting that they would
be retrieved by the butler or the footman.

Sansovino ran twice at Royal Ascot, winning the Prince of Wales
Stakes before being trounced in the Hardwicke Stakes two days

later. His sorrowful owner remarked: "I shall always be just a little afraid in the future of his not putting it all in in a race. With regard to his future I am sure that we must give him a really long rest and I hope that you won't dream of running him before the St Leger."

During the summer Sir Abe Bailey tried to buy Pharos to stand as a stallion in South Africa; Walter Alston became ill and had to undergo an operation; and Sansovino was scratched from the St Leger, leaving the way clear for His Highness the Aga Khan's Salmon Trout to triumph. Lord Derby wrote to Lambton on 3 October congratulating him on the assistance that he had given the Aga Khan in the purchase of bloodstock:

> I did not see you before I went away after the big race yesterday. It was another tribute to the wonderful purchases you have made for the Aga Khan. I am afraid it makes him definitely head of the winning owners and Lady Sykes head of the winning breeders. The running also is a tribute to Tranquil and makes one regret that unfortunate accident to her. She would have swept the board. . . . The whole of the next week I hope to be at Newmarket. We thought, if it suited you, we should shoot on the Thursday as Edward cannot be down there on Wednesday morning. Will you arrange this? The guns would be yourself, Edward, Malcolm, and myself and I think you generally ask Carslake. You could also ask any other gun if you thought that it was necessary.
>
> Do not forget to back Moabite for me whenever you think the time has arrived. Also Edward's bet at the same time.

George Lambton once again became too ill to continue training before the season was over. He went to Cap d'Ail from where he wrote to Lord Derby: "Thanks for making my journey very comfortable and being looked after as if I was a Prince. What a difference it makes. Marvellously the Blue Train arrived at Cap d'Ail to the minute. Sorry to have left the ship before it got to harbour, but I really had got to my limit." Whilst in the South of France he caught flu and Lord Derby, with typical consideration, told him:

> It is a bore that your short holiday should be spoilt in this way – but I hope it is passing off. I really think, however, you ought to consider whether, in view of this, you would not stay out a little longer. If you have to leave the Villa because Billy has someone else coming, you must let me act as your host at an hotel.

Whilst Lambton was away it was arranged to sell Moabite at the December sales. Lord Derby then decided to sell the horse privately, but was forestalled:

> I happened to see Somerville Tattersall at Manchester and hinted to him that I might take Moabite out of the Sale, upon which he pointed out to me that it was in their printed conditions that "whenever a horse is advertised for sale it must not be sold privately before that sale", and apparently, although he was quite nice about it, he would have resented it very much if I had taken him out. So I am afraid there is no alternative, as Tattersall has got such a whiphand of one, and if we offended him we might have great difficulty in getting our horses in a good position for sale another year. I have written to Walter breaking the news to him that I have bought Royal Favour, but that she will be kept at Victoria's, and I want her to go to Phalaris. As I know these changes upset him, if you could you might tell him that the mare is a very nice one, and exaggerate still further and say that you advised me to buy her. I think that will console him for what otherwise I am sure he will think a piece of folly on my part.

Lord Derby gave a party for the stablemen at Stanley House in the week before Christmas, and early in the New Year went to the South of France. The Lambtons had been staying at Eden Rock, and enjoyed a wonderful holiday.

On his return Lord Derby went to Ruthin in North Wales for a health cure:

> The cure is very stringent here, and I have got Victoria to keep me company. I lost 8½ lbs in the first week. They found that there was something very wrong with me. They hope that it will yield to treatment if not I am afraid I shall have to have an operation. However I am hoping for the best.

From Ruthin Lord Derby also wrote:

> I do not know that I ever told you that I wanted to have a sketch of you done by Orpen for the Dining Room at Newmarket. He has consented to do this and I hope you won't object. I did tell Cicely about it. It will only be a sketch and therefore I do not think will require many sittings. He is also painting me for Manchester, but that I am afraid is a more lengthy affair. He has written to say that he will keep free dates between the 25th of April and the 23rd of

May. I have told him I can manage certain dates but I am doubtful whether you will be able to because of the racing, in which case it would have to be postponed till the autumn. Let me know what you think about this.

In a further letter:

I am not getting on any too well though I have lost a little more weight this week. However I shall know my fate more definitely next Tuesday as I am to be X-rayed again when they will decide whether the treatment is having any effect or whether I shall have to have an operation. I think they incline to the belief that the operation may not be necessary though perhaps I take rather a more gloomy view of the situation, but as you can imagine living in a Nursing Home and getting practically nothing to eat and with nothing but lime juice and water to drink is likely to depress one . . .

Three days later Lord Derby reported:

My fate is still undecided but they are going to have a consultation about me on Wednesday when Dawson and the big Leeds surgeon, Sir Berkeley Moynihan, are coming here. I do not feel at all bad in myself, really better in some ways than when I came here and I should think I have lost well over a stone but there is something wrong with me and though the head doctor here assures me it is nothing very bad and that I should soon get over an operation still I hate the idea of an operation at all. However it may be absolutely necessary in which case I should have it done at once.

It had always been customary for racing correspondents to tour stables early in the New Year, and in January 1925 the *Sporting Chronicle* correspondent contributed a graphic description of a go-ahead racing stables in the Twenties, which is worth quoting at length:

Stanley House is really a separate community in itself. There are more than fifty stable lads on the pay roll, and working under ideal conditions they comprise a very happy and united family. Those who live in have separate cubicles, and nothing which conduces to their well-being is missing. The billiards room at Stanley House is as fine a place of its kind as can be seen anywhere, and the comfort of the lads is studied in every possible way.

Mr Lambton is a great believer in healthy sport, and the stable's football team has won the McCalmont Cup many times.

The stables occupy three sides of a rectangle, with numerous additions at the back. There is accommodation for some 80 horses, and the appointments are as up to date as it is possible for them to be. There are four studs included in the estate, the Woodlands, where Swynford and Chaucer stand; the Side Hill, where Phalaris stands; the Plantation, where Stedfast stands and the Hatchfield Farm.

Lord Derby has a private gallop on which he exercises his horses. This is situated opposite the Limekilns, and consists of a moss-litter track. It originally belonged to Sir J. Blundell-Maple, and was subsequently acquired by the Jockey Club. Lambton and Gilpin rented it between them until the war, when it was ploughed up. Lord Derby purchased it last year, and it has now been relaid and considerably improved, with the result that the Stanley House horses will have a very fine gallop for their sole use when a dry spell sets in and the training grounds become hard.

I have said that the comfort of the stable lads is studied in every way, and it goes without saying that the remark applies with equal force to the equine members of the establishment. I was keenly interested in the sand beds used by the horses. It is not every training establishment that possesses one, but Stanley House has three, two of which are out of doors. One of these open-air sand beds is for the colts, and the other for the fillies. The indoor one consists of a big room. Its walls are padded to prevent the possibility of a horse injuring itself, and the sand, which is obtained from the East coast, and changed at intervals, is about a foot and a half deep.

Lambton is a firm believer in the efficacy of the sand bath as a tonic for racehorses, and every one of his charges is let loose into the sand beds every morning on returning from exercise.

The teams commence work very early in the morning. In the summer the first string leaves the stable at six o'clock (five o'clock Greenwich time), returning at 8.30. The second string goes out at ten o'clock and comes back at noon. Both lots of horses are dressed down immediately on their return. At six o'clock every evening Lambton goes round the stable, and inspects each horse in its box in turn.

The stable has a starting gate of its own in one of the paddocks, and a two year old is well schooled under it before being seen in public.

The stable's jockey, Tommy Weston, recently underwent an operation on his tonsils in a Leeds nursing home, but I am glad to say that he is all right again now, and getting himself fit for the coming campaign. There is another "jockey" in the stable in the person of Lambton's daughter, Nancy. She is only 14 years of age, but is frequently to be seen riding one or other of the stable's thoroughbreds at morning exercise on Newmarket Heath. This charming little lady rode the Derby Cup winner, Spindrift, in a lot of the filly's work last year, and combines a perfect seat in the saddle, with beautiful hands.

I have frequently heard the remark passed by people who have seen her riding on the Heath, "what a pity she's not a boy", and this very aptly sums up her skill as a horsewoman. The compliment is no idle one.

Horses roll over and kick about in the sand to their hearts' content, and are afterwards rubbed dry and allowed to graze for a few minutes. All of them have become very fond of this part of their routine, and if there is one in particular in the stable with a keener relish for it than any of the others it is Pharos, who puts an astonishing amount of vim into the exercise. The idea of the sand bath for racehorses originated, I believe, in the United States, and at Stanley House it is one of the most popular of the items in the curriculum.

Another regular feature of the day's work is that at about five o'clock every day, when the weather is fine, each horse is led round one of the paddocks, and is afterwards allowed to graze for ten minutes or so. There is a frame erected in an archway of the stable containing the plates of all horses who have won races for Stanley House, the date, the name of the race, and its value being inscribed in each case. I could not stop to count them, and Lambton may have to get some more frames soon.

The celebrated Isonomy* has an appropriate resting place in the grounds of Stanley House. Sansovino and Swynford, two of the best horses Lambton has trained, both trace back to him. Sansovino was by Swynford, who was by John o'Gaunt. John o'Gaunt was by Isinglass, who was by Isonomy. The Duchess of Montrose put up a plate in memory of Isonomy, and a stone

* Isonomy, who won the 1879 Ascot Gold Cup, Goodwood Cup and Doncaster Cup, sired two Triple Crown winners – Isinglass and Common – before his death in 1891. He had been trained by John Porter at Kingsclere for Mr F. Gretton, a wealthy brewer.

marks his burial place. The grave of another horse, Riviera, is close by.

Pharos and Sansovino were both in training during 1925, although Lord Derby had every intention of keeping Pharos as a stallion. Regarding Sansovino's future, Walter Alston wrote:

As to Sansovino I am strongly of opinion from the point of view of his Stud prospects he had much better go on racing. He seems to be quite honest and after all he beat the 2,000 guineas winner at Lingfield, and if for any reason St Germans had been prevented from running at Epsom * he would have been hailed as a great horse by press and public. There would be no rush for him now at a high fee and he might easily improve his position during the season. I know George agrees in this.

Pharos was still the best horse in the stable, and with the exception of the three-year-old Conquistador, who was unlucky in the Derby, could "do what he likes with our horses". This realization made Lord Derby contemplate introducing fresh blood into his stud, and on the death of Sir Edward Hulton he considered buying the newspaper baron's bloodstock empire:

I can get to hear nothing definite about the Hulton horses. Lady Hulton telegraphed to me to say she would be very glad that I should have the horses, but unfortunately she has gone abroad and will apparently be away for some time. I am trying to get in touch with the other executor, but I am afraid that the sum I should have to offer would be beyond my powers: as although I could sell off a great many of the animals, whether in training or at the stud, people would know that I had taken off the cream, and they would not pay as much for the skimmed milk.

Days later he wrote to Lambton:

Please don't forget, if you look at Hulton's mares, to look particularly at Fifine and Soubriquet. These are the two which I think of bidding for. Apparently Harry Greer has received no instructions to buy for the Aga Khan so it is quite possible prices may not be as high as we thought.

---

* In the Coronation Cup St Germans had beaten Sansovino by six lengths, with the third horse, Plack, four lengths behind Sansovino.

George Lambton told Lord Derby on 10 July:

> I have seen Hulton's mares; Soubriquet is as good a mare as you
> could see and worth a lot of money and she will bring a big price
> . . . I liked Silver and her foal and also a very good foal by
> Tetratema from Fifinella . . . Colorado's legs are first rate but he
> has had one or two eruptions on his body. . . . Sansovino is
> cantering again and moves well, but that bony enlargement will
> never go down, but will probably get callous. Willie Waugh
> asked if he was for sale and said that the Italians would give us a
> big price. I must say I do not like him as a stallion.

Lord Derby returned to Ruthin in early August, and wrote from
Gullane ten days later: "I really had a very successful time – did not
lose as much weight as last time but lost 16 lbs, and am feeling very
fit and well . . . I am now playing golf every day and all day." (He
loved the "Royal and Ancient" game, even though he was never
better than a long handicap player whose unorthodox style caused
the club to hit the back of his neck at the top of his swing. He
possessed his own golf course at Swinley Forset near Ascot; employed his own golf professional, and at Gullane where he spent
much of September each year, he had the crest of a small hill
removed to make his walk along one of the fairways less arduous.)
Despite the enjoyment of his golf he complained to Lambton about
the handicapping of his horses:

> I have a great mind to complain of Lee's handicapping at Doncas-
> ter. He wants to get his knife into me as I am one of the Stewards
> at Hurst Park, Kempton and Liverpool, all of which have told
> him that they are not going to continue to employ him. I am
> sorry for him in some ways, but he really is too bad now.

In October Pharos was taken out of training and sent to the
Woodland Stud, but Sansovino remained in training and Lambton
thought that he might run him in the Cambridgeshire, for "I cannot
see that his reputation is going to suffer from running him in the big
handicap with his big weight and it is just possible that he might
regain his reputation – all the same I should fancy him more on a
round course."

At the end of the month George Lambton had a fall and on 24
October Cicely wrote:

> My dear Lord Derby,
>   George has asked me to write to you as he is staying in bed

today, it is most fearful bad luck. Last night at stable time he walked out of the office in a hurry – he was on his way to go round 2nd lot – it was a pitch dark night and Murland switched the lights in the office out just at that moment. George turned sharp right-handed thinking he was walking through the opening but instead of that he must have missed it, and caught his knees on the little low wall, with the result that as he was walking rather fast he went headlong onto the concrete outside the boxes. He has cut his head open rather badly and has had to have stitches put into it. Luckily he was not concussed at all and not knocked out for more than a moment . . . he is keeping quiet today and will not go to Sandown tomorrow. Osgood picked up a big flint just about where he fell which must have been the cause of the cut . . .

The injury caused George Lambton to write to Lord Derby about his future, and again thoughts of retirement entered his mind. Lord Derby answered his letter by return of post, discussing the possibility of Frank Butters eventually training the Stanley House horses – a possibility which had already been proposed to Butters with the approval of George Lambton, who was contemplating the end of the 1926 season as the most suitable time to relinquish training.

Fifty-year-old Frank Butters seemed a sensible choice to take over from George Lambton, for he had more than two decades of training experience in Austria and Italy and came from a family steeped in racing. His mother was a daughter of James Waugh and his father, Joseph, who had been born on the Knowsley Estate in 1847, had been apprenticed to John Scott, whose patrons included the 14th Earl of Derby. Subsequently Joseph Butters rode for the Emperor Franz Joseph and trained in Austria before returning to Newmarket in 1903. Nevertheless despite his experience it was obvious that Frank Butters would have a difficult and unenviable task in attempting to follow in the footsteps of George Lambton, particularly as Lambton would be breathing down his neck and constantly criticizing his training methods, even though these methods had brought him considerable success in Italy since the end of the First World War.

Lord Derby elaborated his views to Lambton about his future and that of Butters:

I am very glad you should have written frankly. It is just what I wanted you to do. I will deal first of all with your remarks about Butters.

I quite agree that the commencement of 1928 seems a long way off but it really was your own suggestion that there should be a year in which there should be no binding agreement between us when Butters might go about to see different race courses etc and get to know about racing generally, whilst the second year he should be definitely assistant trainer. Needless to say I want to put off the day when you actually give up training as long as possible but if you think that should be before January 1928 so be it. The only thing that I think is essential is that some definite date should be fixed. Nothing would be more likely to prevent Butters taking the post than the date of his taking over being indefinite. If therefore you wish the change to take place at the end of 1926 well and good but it is you and not I who will say the word.

Now with regard to yourself. What I suggested I thought was in your interests as I felt that the time might come when you were still able to manage the Stable but could not stand the fatigue of Sales like the Newmarket and Doncaster ones. I cannot pretend to put myself in the way of expenditure on a footing with the Aga Khan and I do not think that you would wish your position as Manager of the Stable to be analogous to that of Dudley Gilroy or Featherstonhaugh.★ It is quite true they are both of them allowed to undertake other work but you must remember that if I am rightly informed they only get £1,200 a year and no house. I only mention this to show you that I was not only thinking of my own interests but also of yours. But you may be quite sure that I should never let money difficulties come between us and once it is arranged about Butters then you need have no fear that we shall not together make your financial arrangements satisfactory to you.

The whole question therefore to my mind devolves on Butters and whether he will accept or not and I think the best way I can leave it is this that you should see him and see on what terms he would be prepared to come rather than that I should suggest terms to him through you. The only thing that I think must be definite is as I have said the actual date on which he should be able to count on taking over from you.

I am coming down to Newmarket but fear I may not get down till Tuesday morning and shall be able to stay till Thursday. We could have a good talk Tuesday night after the Sales and if everything is satisfactory I could see Butters and clinch matters with him on the Wednesday.

★ Racing manager to King George V.

Edward Stanley, the future
17th Earl of Derby, in 1896

The Hon. George Lambton at
Bedford Lodge in 1908

Cicely Horner at the time of her marriage to the Hon. George Lambton, December 1908

Knowsley – Lord Derby's home at Prescot near Liverpool

Lord Derby leading in Swynford (Frank Wootton) after his 1910 St Leger victory

Lord Derby's daughter, Lady Victoria Bullock, and the Hon. Mrs George Lambton at the races in 1925

Cicely Lambton watches Lord Derby admiring Pharos after the colt's six-length victory in the Duke of York Handicap at Kempton in 1925

The Hon. George Lambton with his seven-year-old son Teddy in 1925

Lady Derby and Cicely Lambton at the 1927 St Leger meeting at Doncaster

The Hon. George Lambton – from a
painting by Lynwood Palmer

George and Cicely Lambton with Michael and Eve Beary and General
'Perry' Harding and his wife Liz (sitting on the gate) at Newmarket in 1942

Lord Derby's 1933 Christmas card – leading in Hyperion after his Derby triumph

George Lambton expressed his thoughts on his possible retirement in a practical letter:

I can get Wynards Lodge for a year and am going over it tomorrow. The proprietors want to sell for £2,500. I believe that Lady Curzon wants to buy a house, perhaps Falmouth House would do for her if you want to sell. About Osgood. I talked it over with Butters and think it would not be advisable to turn him out of his house this year especially as he is still acting head lad for me, and as he is anxious for him to continue in the same place with him it would not start the connection in a tactful manner. I do not think it is at all likely that Osgood would think of starting training himself, to begin with I am sure that he has not enough money, also I am sure that he would not like giving up a job in which he has spent the best years of his life. There never has been a more devoted and loyal servant. I sometimes think you have never quite appreciated what a large part he has played in the fortunes of Stanley House for many years. I have little doubt that he and Butters will get on, but there is the house difficulty, and I am afraid that Falmouth Cottage might be a bit too far for a head lad.

Before Christmas Lord Derby wrote:

I think that the best present to give each of the men is a cardigan. Would you get them and give them in both Alice's and my name? I thought I would also give them a dinner – just before the beginning of the Flat Season. If you can tear yourself away from hunting you must come out to the South of France and stay with me.

(Lord Derby had bought a villa above Cannes which he named Sansovino after his colt's victory, and which was to provide a winter retreat for much of January each year.)

In February 1926 Frank Butters arrived in England and discussed his future with Lord Derby, who returned to Cannes the next day seemingly satisfied that Butters would be an adequate successor to George Lambton.

George Lambton was now enjoying his start as a journalist and contributed an article to *English Life* on jockeys, in which he wrote:

Jockeys of to-day are for the most part much smaller men than their predecessors, and, consequently, their physical privations are not so severe. They do not walk enough, they do not ride enough, and are partly the victims of the age, when motor-cars have made life luxurious and easy, and it is more usual in these days to see a jockey on a motor-cycle or in a car than on a hack. In the winter, when racing is over, the last thing the majority of them ever do is to get on a horse. That is why, although there are quite a number of pretty good jockeys, the younger ones amongst them are terribly deficient in horsemanship.

Touching on the question of excessive cigarette smoking, he wrote:

The most successful jockeys have been very light smokers; surely that should be an example and a lesson to an ambitious boy. I am strongly of opinion that neither smoking nor drinking should be allowed in the jockeys' dressing rooms. It is such a thoroughly bad example for the younger boys, and the evil of it cannot be exaggerated. The Jockey Club should take the matter in hand. There can be no valid reason against their making some rule to prevent it.

8

Lambton – the Manager

Throughout the summer of 1926 the General Strike caused havoc with racing – as did the proposed Betting Tax introduced by the Chancellor of the Exchequer, Mr Winston Churchill, which resulted in *The Times* publishing leading articles with banner headlines such as "Proposal both ruinous and impossible" and "Horse-breeding in Peril". However the season had started auspiciously for Stanley House, and Lord Derby had won the Two Thousand Guineas with Colorado, ridden by Tommy Weston. Five weeks later they had finished third to Coronach in The Derby on an appalling afternoon when torrential rain soaked the course. Soon after the Epsom meeting Colorado developed a form of rheumatism, and there was no possibility of him being kept in training after Ascot. Luckily Caissot, out of Lord Derby's Classic winning mare Keysoe, was thought to be a worthy substitute for the St Leger, although the question of a jockey was causing concern, due to the fact that Weston, on his own admission, did not get on with Caissot. Eventually Carslake took the mount, but they came second to Coronach, who once again showed his superiority.

George Lambton retired as a trainer at the end of the 1926 season, but there were still many items about which Lord Derby wished to consult him in his capacity of manager of his horses. One was the subject of hacks:

> Hacks. As you will realize, things are rather different with Butters than they were with you. Butters, as you told me, is not much of a horseman, and he had better buy with your help his own hacks, and enough for the other men. I should pay for them, and they would be mine. But you will want a hack or two. I know you like having your own so I would either keep them for you or perhaps you would prefer to keep them with your other horses and with Cicely's hacks and the children's ponies.

A month later came a further letter, written from the Villa Sansovino, about his duties as a manager:

Forgive me for not having written before. It has been so lovely here that I have played golf all day, and been too lazy to write in the evening.

I quite agree with you as to the duties of a manager. You are responsible for the entries and for the running of the horses as you think fit. Butters is responsible for the training and as far as I am concerned I suppose you will write to me as to your intentions about running and the chances of the horses, and Butters will write to me as to how they are.

Sorry to see in the *Sporting Life* your leg is still bad and you can't hunt. Why not come out here?

Best of luck for 1927.

"Best of luck" not only referred to high hopes for the Stanley House horses, but also to George Lambton's new career as a racing journalist. However Lord Derby felt obliged to point out:

There is only one thing I do ask and that is that in any articles you may write you do not refer to our horses either as regards their future or as to their past running. In other words anything you may say about horses shall be dealing with horses of the past and not the horses of the present.

In midsummer 1927 Call Boy, owned by theatrical impresario Frank Curzon, won The Derby, but less than a month later Curzon was dead. It was suggested that Lord Derby should buy the Epsom hero, of whom Lambton thought little. Derby wrote to him:

With regard to Call Boy I do not quite know what to do. Walter is anxious that I should buy him as he thinks he would nick very well with our mares and I am prepared to do so provided he does not go for any very extravagant price. I have suggested to Walter to talk to you and then to make judicious enquiries as to price, etc. I should think £40,000 ought to buy him. If it did I think I should be prepared to give it. I should have to borrow the money, insure the horse, make a sinking fund, etc., but I think on the whole at that price he would pay me, or at all events I should not be a loser.

During July George Lambton was thinking about his son's future, and wrote to Lord Derby:

You remember me talking to you about John and his future. The regiment I want to get him into is the 11th Hussars which is, I believe, the Duke of York's regiment, and they say one has to get his influence. If you could do anything it would be very kind.

Lord Derby replied:

I am writing to the War Office about John, to find out what the proper course is, and will let you know. If, as you think, the Duke of York is the honorary Colonel of the Regiment, then you could write to him direct, or I would do so if you wished. Probably the best thing would be for you to write him a letter and for me to send it on with a covering letter, asking him to put John's name down on his list. However, I will let you know in a few days definitely what is to be done.

Rumours were rife at the time that villainy was being perpetrated on racecourses and Lambton mentioned to Lord Derby (27 August):

Weston has just blown in . . . he says that there is no doubt, whatever, that the story he tells is true; that horses have been got at in the northern circuit by these two men, and that it is done as he described to you. I asked him how he first came to hear about it but I could not get the names of the two men who told him – so far as I can make out he is not going to disclose their names unless matters really get going. . . . Weston is a determined little fellow and not easy to move . . . and I have no doubt in my own mind that Weston is taking considerable risks himself. He also says that Bogside and Lanark are the easy places for these people to work.

On a more light-hearted note Lambton mentioned to Lord Derby: "The damned porter at Crewe put me on the wrong portion of the train yesterday, and I swept past Rugby – no stop until Euston, and I had asked the man particularly if I was all right for Rugby!"
Lord Derby was amused by the porter's incompetence and in his reply suggested another journey:

If you are going to York I wish you would go over if you can to see the Thornton Stud. It would not take you long in a motor. I would rather like to have your candid opinion about it. Personally I think it could be made into a very nice Stud. There is heaps of room, and we do want some sort of isolation place. Of course we have got bad mares there now, though I believe some of the

better barren ones are to go up there later. . . . Walter has got a
great down on Thornton, which I think is rather undeserved.

In the autumn Lord Derby was "cock-a-hoop" at the success of
his two-year-old Kantar in France. The colt was unbeaten in four
races, including the valuable and prestigious Prix Morny and Grand
Critérium, and consequently he insisted that George Lambton
should pay a special visit to France to inspect Kantar:

> They are very keen for you to see the horses at Chantilly . . . if
> you like to take your servant, please do. I want you to look
> carefully at the horses and let me know exactly what you think
> when you get back . . . If I were you I should take as much
> luggage as you can with you in the compartment, as it would save
> your having to go through the Customs with the big luggage
> afterwards. The Golden Arrow is a wonderful train.

As expected, Lambton enjoyed his trip to Paris and reported
favourably upon the Derby horses at Chantilly under the care of
Saint-Sauveur and Carver.

Unhappily, personal tragedy for Lord Derby was not far distant.
In November 1927 he was stunned by the death of his daughter
Victoria. Staying with Lord and Lady Blandford at Lowesby Hall
in Leicestershire to hunt with the Quorn, she died from
injuries received when her horse took fright whilst being ridden
under a low narrow railway bridge which had an iron bar at
either end. She raised her head too soon, fractured her skull and died
the following day without regaining consciousness. At the time of
the accident her father was en route for the South of France. He was
told the sad news by a British Embassy official when he arrived at
the Gare du Nord in Paris. He was very fond of his son-in-law
Malcolm Bullock and wrote to him: "I cannot talk or write to you
about her, I am too great a coward, but I loved her as no man has
ever loved his daughter, and with her has gone all joy from my
life . . ."

A month later, on 4 December, Lord Derby wrote to Lambton
about Schiavoni (Swynford-Serenissima), who had won the Liverpool Spring Cup before becoming difficult to train:

> I do not know whether Edward has written to you with regard to
> Schiavoni. There has been rather a mistake made. I made en-
> quiries of the British Bloodstock Agency to find out whether
> Schiavoni would do for Trinidad. Apparently the Colony took

that as being an offer of the horse from me and the Governor has written gratefully accepting. I feel that under the circumstances I ought to withdraw him from the Sale and send him out to them. If you agree and if Tattersall does not raise any objection, as I do not think he will when the circumstances are explained to him, would you arrange with the British Bloodstock Agency to take charge of him and to send him out? The Governor tells me that they will undertake all expenses.

By Christmas, Fairway (by Phalaris–Scapa Flow), who had achieved considerable success as a two-year-old, was pleasing Lambton, who wrote:

He has improved more than I thought possible since October and is now a really beautiful horse, he has darkened in colour very much, and you can now see some likeness to Pharos, which he never showed before. His leg has improved as much as the rest of him, and the knot in his tendon has gone – and that was what frightened me . . . many thanks for the presents for the children which they are delighted with – and no wonder . . .

Throughout the winter Fairway continued to satisfy Lambton, who stated in an article published in early April 1928:

Fairway does not resemble his full-brother Pharos in any way except that he has the same beautiful head and intelligent eye. He has taken after his grandsire, Polymelus, more than his sire, Phalaris, and is a light-framed colt that in the early part of the season may be difficult to train. I can foresee some anxious moments for Frank Butters.

He told Lord Derby:

Polymelus and Phalaris, as three-year-olds, were neither of them able to produce their best form early in the year, but they both kept on steadily improving with age, and I expect Fairway to do the same.

There is some prejudice against the stock of Phalaris with regard to stamina, but I have no fear of the mile and a half at Epsom being beyond Fairway's powers.

On the final day of March Lambton had explained to Lord Derby:

I expect Fairway to win the Two Thousand Guineas although he has not had good horses to gallop with, and we have only his style of going to make one think him a good horse . . . about backing Fairway for The Derby it has been almost impossible at a decent price. Falcon got me £5500 to £500 – you said you would like £200 or £300 I forget which – would you like it or would you prefer to wait. Of course if he gets beat for the 2000 he will be easier to back – if he wins impossible.

Fairway did not contest the Two Thousand Guineas because of boils in his mouth, but made a winning début at the second spring meeting at Newmarket, when he won with ease and authority – a victory which caused his price for The Derby to shorten and the bookmakers to install him as favourite. However, despite George Lambton's pleasure at the prospect of Fairway winning at Epsom, he was compelled to turn his attention to family matters when his eldest brother was taken seriously ill. "I was called up at 2.0 last night," he informed Lord Derby.

The doctor told me that Jack was ill – when I got here he was fighting for life. Heart failure. The doctor had very little hope. However at about 4.0 he took a turn for the better and has since steadily gained ground but of course there is still a certain amount of danger and I do not like to go away. I am glad to say that Cicely is much better although she is still in bed. However I will come on Saturday but am bringing my servant as Cicely thinks I shall die without him.

At this time Lord Derby was telling Lambton his future racing plans:

I had luncheon with Walter and a long and very satisfactory talk with him. He looks very ill and there is nothing of him but at the same time he is in very good spirits. I broached the subject of dividing the Stud into 3, the Newmarket Stud, the French Stud and Thornton. He quite agrees about the French Stud and about the Thornton Stud, although at first he was rather suspicious of it, at the end I think he approved the principle.

What I suggested was this. A certain number of mares should be sent definitely to Thornton which should be their headquarters, although at any time we might make a transfer between one of the mares there and one of the mares at Newmarket. The mares at Newmarket to be the absolutely first class ones. The ones at Thornton to be the 2nd class maiden mares and mares about whose produce we were a little doubtful and wanted to give them another chance.

I suggested that the man at Thornton should have complete charge making suggestions to Walter as to how the mares should be mated and taking his orders on that point from him, but that after the mating had been settled Walter should no longer be bothered with the arrangements.

Now with regard to the matter of the writing of articles by trainers which was mentioned at the Jockey Club. It was a desultory conversation in which I took some part. Your name was mentioned but quite from a different point of view from that which you think. Your articles were referred to as having been written by a trainer who is now a manager and therefore holding no licence from the Jockey Club, which is a very different thing from a licensed trainer. Your case was quoted as being that of a man who wrote about past history and very different from some of the articles that are being written at the present moment. There is no doubt, between ourselves, that the man aimed at was Vandy Beatty although his name was not mentioned. The Stewards are going to take some action and I think rather on the lines that I suggested, that they deprecate the giving of tips, which is what it amounts to, by trainers holding a licence and that if it is continued the writers' applications for licences next year will not be favourably considered. As far as I am concerned I have not the least objection to your continuing writing in the press on the lines that you are writing at the present moment.

Although Fairway started a short-priced favourite for The Derby he was not placed behind Felstead, for he became thoroughly upset in the preliminaries due to the behaviour of those who crowded round him, anxious to get a close view of the supposed champion. George Lambton had motored to Epsom at dawn to watch the early morning gallop of Fairway. On the return journey to London before breakfast he ruefully told his chauffeur that Fairway would not win, but never elaborated upon this comment, which was proved correct later in the day.

To compensate for this disappointment, Toboggan won The Oaks, and a delighted Lord Derby wrote to Lambton on 12 June:

I want to consult you about presents for Toboggan winning. I shall be sending you yours, £500, and I want to know whether you consider the following fair:

Butters and Weston each £500 (They of course get a percentage in addition)

Osgood £50

Stables and Private Ground men to be distributed by Butters £150

Just let me have a line to say whether you think this is all right. Of course I shall send separately to Walter Alston and to the men at the Stud.

Tell me perfectly frankly if you don't think the presents are sufficient. I am basing it very much on the Eclipse of last year although of course the amount of The Oaks is a good bit less than the Eclipse.

In midsummer 1928 George Lambton wrote from Overstrand Hall, Cromer: "Jack has been bad again, very high blood pressure, and I am taking him back to Newmarket today. He is in a bad way and I do not think that he can last very long – any one of these attacks might be the end, and for his own sake I shall not be sorry when it comes." Less than a month later he told Lord Derby (20 September): "Jack died very peacefully early this morning, he had been unconscious for twenty-four hours and had no pain – I could not have wished him to continue the hopeless struggle any longer."

The Earl of Durham had suffered many sorrows in his life, the most grievous being the illness of his wife, Ethel, a grand-daughter of Sir William Mordaunt Milner of Nunappleton Hall, York. Less than three years after their wedding Lord Durham applied for an application of nullity on the grounds that his wife was of unsound mind at the time of the marriage. The hearing lasted a week, but Lord Durham was considered not to have established his case. Tragically the mental disorder from which his wife was suffering proved incurable, but the marriage remained valid.

Fairway redeemed his reputation by winning the Eclipse, and then won the St Leger to credit Lord Derby with his fourth Doncaster Classic – one more than any other owner had ever achieved. This triumph upset the theory that a Phalaris colt could not stay $14\frac{1}{2}$ furlongs – a theory which Pharos and Colorado had failed to disprove. Lambton had always thought Fairway was a great horse because of his action, his character, his appearance and the style with which he won both his home trials and his races. At home Fairway was never asked a "big question" on the gallops either as a two-year-old or a three-year-old.

At Longchamp in October Kantar, owned jointly by Lord Derby

and the American Mr Ogden Mills, the father of Lady Granard, won the Prix de l'Arc de Triomphe to give the Stanley House colours their most important success on the French Turf. The partners had bought Kantar in a batch of yearlings from M. E. de Saint Alary for 2,200,000 francs.* Neither Lord Derby nor Mr Ogden Mills, who was to die three months later, was present to see their colt's Longchamp victory, but George Lambton witnessed it, and backed him to win a considerable sum. It was a great year in France for Lord Derby, as earlier in the summer the Grand Prix de Paris had been won by Cri de Guerre, whom he also owned in partnership with Mr Ogden Mills.

The 1929 season began inauspiciously, but at Whitsun Lord Derby wrote (21 May) and gave news of his house-party for Epsom week:

> I may go and see Bosworth run tomorrow† but I am not sure that I ought to owing to Rosebery's death. I am going to talk the matter over with Alice. . . .
>
> Don't forget you and Cicely are coming to Coworth though I am afraid you may be horribly bored with only Alice and Malcolm and myself there. I daresay it is possible we may find somebody else who wants a bed and dinner. Beatrix Granard and Saint Sauveur are coming for one night.

This letter was followed up by another (3 June) giving details of Epsom arrangements, and adding: "I hope your gout is better because I am firmly convinced that it is gout and I saw last night that Cicely shared my opinion."

Royal Ascot brought a triumph for Fairway in the Rous Memorial Stakes but no success with Lord Derby's other six runners, and twenty-four hours after his victory Lord Derby wrote (22 June):

> Now with regard to last week. I was very disappointed with the running of our horses with the exception of Fairway and am rather depressed at the outlook.
>
> My disappointment was two-fold. First the number of our horses that ran and secondly the way in which they ran. If you take the number of horses we have in training and the number that have been on a racecourse this year you will see that it is only a very small percentage and this week at Ascot showed me very

---

* About £17,000, for there were approximately 130 francs to the pound.
† Royal Standard Stakes, Manchester Whitsun meeting.

clearly that even those that do run are very far from being fit. Bosworth, Sargasso, Knight of Lorne, and Fair Isle, all very backward and as far as I can see, and from what you and Butters tell me, the other horses are even more backward.

In July John Lambton was gazetted into the West Yorkshire Foot Regiment. Referring to this commission George Lambton told Lord Derby: "they say that he did not pass out high enough to get a Cavalry commission – a damned nuisance. Of course it is his own fault for not working harder – and I think he will probably have a poor life there."

Lord Derby was not entirely happy with Butters and wrote a draft letter to him suggesting that his position at Stanley House might be terminated. Typically he sent the draft to George Lambton for his criticism and comments. Lambton replied:

> I return your letters – there are one or two things which perhaps might be improved. I don't quite like "although we have had our disappointments" and I am not sure of "I will do everything in my power to get you new patrons". I should end the letter something like this, with perhaps a little more human touch, otherwise your letter reads to me a little cold. "It goes to my heart that circumstances should force me to take this step, and if there is anything that I can do to lessen what I know must be a most serious blow to you, you can rely upon all the help that I can give you". I feel that it is impertinent in my suggesting improvements in your letter as no one can do these things better than you, – but here your heart has not been in the letter, and you have not been able to come out as you usually do.

Lord Derby commented:

> I got your two letters today for which many thanks, though they were most depressing reading, and I do not think we have ever had the stable so full of sick and crocked up horses. Everything tends to prove that Butters is quite incapable of training a big stable. I do not know what we are to do. I feel that one will probably have to give him a chance again next year, but if he does not do better next year I shall certainly make a change. We cannot go on like this. He is doing just what you say, not giving the horses enough slow work when the ground is hard, and then rushing at them as soon as it begins to get soft, and breaking them down.

I am not sure that the thing which disturbs me most is not the fact that so many of our mares are breeding unsound animals – Selene, Spindrift, Tranquil, Keysoe; and others breeding bad animals – Fifine and Whitewash.

I have had this morning almost simultaneously telegrams to say that Colorado has had a very bad attack and is not likely to live, and that Hunter's Moon has broken down. I suppose it is as well to get all one's troubles over at the same time, but both these are rather blows, the first especially.

Of course, if Colorado does die I think it will alter all our plans for Fairway, and we shall have to send him to the Stud next year. There will be time, however, to talk it all over with you in the autumn.

Meanwhile, our outlook is not rosy, either for the immediate future or indeed for next year. . . .

Colorado is certainly making a most gallant struggle, and although one hardly dare hope, still there is no doubt yesterday he was slightly better and was able to go out in the paddock. The curious thing is that just by chance Paine took up an orange. The horse took to it at once, and is now eating two or three of them a day, but will only take them from Paine.

About Bosworth. What do you think about backing him? I see he is at 100 to 8 and if you could get me 2,500 to 200 I would like to take it. Can you do this for me? also let me know what you think of Fairway, as Butters does not write very optimistically about him. I want if possible to avoid his being beaten again, and if he is not going on in the right way it might be as well to take him out of training at once and let him go to the Stud.

But Colorado was still giving anxiety:

I am afraid there is no hope for poor Colorado. Paine telephoned me this morning to say he was getting much weaker, although in other ways he seemed slightly better. It is one of the greatest blows we could have had . . .

The only thing of importance now is John. The West Yorks is a very good regiment, but I quite agree with you that it probably would not suit John. I do not know where either of the battalions are at the present moment, but do not on any account let him chuck up his commission. I do not understand their not giving him a Cavalry commission, as I did not think there were so many candidates for these commissions that they could afford to pick and choose. If you like I would write to the Military Secretary. Tell me which of the Cavalry Regiments he wants to get into . . .

Lambton's plans to go to Scotland after the St Leger, in which Bosworth finished second to Derby winner Trigo, were altered by the death of his brother Hedworth. Nine months earlier Jack Lambton's twin brother Frederick, who had succeeded him as the 4th Earl of Durham, had died – so that three of George Lambton's brothers had died within twelve months. He sent a telegram to Lord Derby: "Just heard of Hedworth's death. I am afraid I must go back tonight to London. So very sorry."

Hedworth Lambton had been Commander-in-Chief of the Royal Navy's China Station in the first decade of the twentieth century, and soon after his return to England in 1910 became the beneficiary of a very substantial fortune. He and his wife, the widow of Viscount Chelsea, were living in a house on the estate of Lady Meux at Theobalds Park near Waltham Cross, Essex. Lady Meux was very fond of Hedworth and his wife, and in her Will she bequeathed her interest in Meux's Brewery and the residue of her estate which included houses in London and a château in France on the condition that he changed his name to Meux. He accepted the condition, and when he died left unsettled property valued at £910,465. George Lambton was also a great personal friend of Lady Meux, who knew that if she had asked him to change his surname she would have received a curt negative reply!

Lord Derby sent his condolences to George Lambton from Gullane on 21 September 1929:

> It was a great shock when we got the message about Hedworth, as although one always expected his death at any time, there had been no sort of warning. In fact I got a letter from Mildred written the night before he died, condoling with me about Colorado, and saying nothing whatever about Hedworth.
>
> I have telegraphed to say I am coming up for the funeral which Portia says is to be at Theobalds. Would you and Cicely have luncheon with me at Claridges; and as there will probably be others there too I should be very glad if you could arrange to come round with me to Derby House afterwards to talk over things, as there are several things I should like to settle with you.

After the Prix de l'Arc de Triomphe, in which his colt Kantar finished second to Ortello, Lord Derby told Lambton:

> Got back last night. We were beaten I think very unluckily in the big race. People will tell you that Esling waited too long and on the face of it it looks like that but the real truth was that a whole lot

of beaten horses fell back at the same time; closed in on him and he could not get through till too late. He was catching the others hand over fist. It is Kantar's last race and I wish he could have won it.

Throughout the winter Lord Derby was having further doubts about Butters' ability as his trainer. To some extent the truth was that he had become so used to dealing with George Lambton, who was his social equal, that he found it difficult to find the correct wavelength when dealing with a trainer who expected to be treated as an employee. His doubts made him more than ever convinced that George Lambton should become even more involved in the day-to-day management of the stables. As a result, by midsummer 1930 he was telling Lambton (13 June):

> I am off to Berlin tomorrow morning, and shall hope to see you at Coworth for dinner on Monday. It is all very tiresome and worrying about Butters, and it puzzles me very much what is the right thing to do, – but we can talk it over next week.
>
> I think you will find Ascot in really good condition; plenty of grass; it may be getting a little hard, but they are steadily watering it I believe the whole way round, and the Cup Course is sure to be good going so I hope Bosworth will stride out.
>
> I get so little racing now that I should like to see as many run as possible.

To his great pleasure Bosworth* won the Ascot Gold Cup, and on 22 June he wrote:

> I can't tell you how pleased I was at winning the Cup. I had always wanted to, but had felt that with Fairway lay my only chance. It was splendid, and really it was better than winning with Fairway, as it has "made" Bosworth, who will suit more of our mares than Fairway will.

But Lord Derby had an even more important matter on his mind. He and George Lambton were now agreed that Lambton would

---

* Lord Derby had given his colt the name Bosworth at the request of his father's only sister, who had been keen on racing until her death at the age of ninety-three. She had continually beseeched him to name a promising colt "Bosworth" to commemorate the battle from whence the title "Lord Derby" came to the Stanley family. Bosworth was a half-brother to Selene and Tranquil.

once again become private trainer at Stanley House. This necessitated giving unpalatable news to Frank Butters, and Lord Derby
told Lambton:

> Thank heavens, we have got over the first fence. I do not know
> when I have disliked a job much more – I meant to have told
> Frank Sunday night after stables, but first Weston and then
> Reynolds came into the office and then it was so late that I
> cowardly took the chance of not saying anything, and writing to
> him, and gave it to him this morning early, before he got yours.
> Of course there is no use disguising the fact that it was a terrible
> shock and surprise to him, and when I saw him later he had not
> got much to say, and it was not easy for me to say any more
> except that I was terribly sorry that circumstances made it
> impossible for you to go on in this same way. He was a little sulky
> but on the whole he took it as well, if not better, than most people
> would have done. Fortunately this afternoon there was a cricket
> match, "Fathers against Sons", and he carried his bat in both
> innings, and he was so pleased that it took a lot of trouble off his
> mind for the moment . . . I had a letter from Walter this
> afternoon: "I wonder if Butters has any idea of what is coming to
> him, he must unless he is devoid of intelligence." I think it ought
> to be made public as soon as possible for his sake, and he thinks
> so, to give him a chance. I think no man would do it better than
> Galtrey in the *Daily Telegraph*. If you think anything of this you
> could send me a wire, and I could tell him – just the fact that the
> stable must be reduced, and that under the circumstances Frank
> Butters will be looking for another job and that nothing else is
> settled – or you might write to Galtrey yourself.

The letter sent by Lord Derby to Butters stated:

> It distresses me as much to write this letter as I am sure it will do
> for you to receive it.
>   Since the imposition of the new and very heavy taxation I have
> been obliged to go most carefully into everything and economise
> in every direction that I can, and I have had to consider most
> carefully the racing expenses. These are very heavy, but up to
> now thanks to the stallions' fees, receipts have just about balanced
> outgoings. But the death of Stedfast, Swynford and Colorado
> and the extra tax on stallions' fees turn the scale, and there is no
> doubt that this year I shall be on the wrong side. Nor can I reckon
> on Fairways and Bosworths every year to keep up the Stable
> income. I have therefore to make extensive reductions, and I can

only do this by cutting down, not only the mares at the Stud, but the horses in training.

I had intended when I succeeded my Father to have a much smaller stable than I now have, and never to have more than five and twenty horses in training. This number has gradually grown, but I now perforce have to bring it down as near as possible to the original number contemplated.

With a much smaller Stable it will be quite impossible for me to keep a high salaried Trainer and Manager, and you will readily understand that, with my long connection with Mr Lambton it is impossible for me in making my choice between the two to avoid retaining him. He will remain as Manager, and he feels that with a smaller Stable he will be able, at all events for a year or so, to carry on with some much smaller salaried assistant than a regular trainer.

I am sorry to say therefore that at the end of the year I must terminate your engagement. I regret this more than I can say.

Although we have had disappointments during the time you have trained for me, we can on the other hand look back on many races both big and small won by our horses, and I am grateful to you for the loyal way in which I know you have always worked for my interest.

You may rest assured that I will do everything in my power either to get you new patrons in this country, or if you prefer to return to Italy to assist you in so doing.

Butters immediately contacted Lord Derby, who informed George Lambton:

Butters has taken my letter extraordinarily well. Naturally it is a tremendous blow and it is quite evident it was entirely unexpected. He is keeping the news confidential for the present, but naturally he would like it to be known that he is setting up as a trainer, and he wants to know the best way of doing it, and whether he should do it through his brother. This I think is a good idea, but how to put it puzzles me very much indeed. I have always felt that the great difficulty in saying I was making the change on the ground of economy was that the Press and perhaps other people would say, "If you want to economize why not have a trainer and not a manager," and if I was asked that I should have to tell them the real reason for getting rid of Butters, which is the last thing I want to do. I hope therefore in his own interest Butters will prevent his brother getting up any sort of agitation. I leave it to you to discuss with him how the announcement can best be made, but in a separate letter that I am putting in this, and which you can show to Butters, I give you my idea.

I have not the slightest doubt that Fairway, Caerleon and Bosworth would still be in training if it had not been for this absolute lack of knowledge on Butters' part. He seems to have taken it very well when you told him, and I am sorry for him. If he sets up himself as a trainer I should be inclined to send him two or three horses.

This letter was followed up by:

I agree with you that playing the hypocrite is a very disagreeable role, and one of our chief difficulties is to come, when we have to say what we are going to do next year. However, we can keep that perfectly quiet, but as I have written to Edward the one thing we must try and aim at is an amalgamation with some stable, with a trainer who has got a nice lot of people training with him whom one would not object to have in. If one simply appointed a trainer and then got people in it would at once be evident that we had really made the change not for economy's sake but to get rid of Butters. I am afraid, poor chap, he is going to have a hard enough job without making it any more difficult for him.

I have been looking through the list of trainers with whom one's friends are training. Of course Cecil★ stands out, but I doubt the possibility of that arrangement coming off. There is another man and that is Victor Gilpin. He has only got Wool-avington, who I think would be quite willing not to send horses to him; (I think he only did it out of kindness to Gilpin); Giles Loder whom I like, and Saint Alary, who is a personal friend of mine. An amalgamation there might be possible. Judging by the number of winners he turns out he seems to be a pretty good trainer.

No, I have got absolutely no remorse about Butters. Although it was a very disagreeable thing to have to do to get rid of him, directly I heard that the vet at Liverpool had said there was no question of a chill with Bosworth, simply that the horse was so over-tired that he was ill I had really no pity for him.

I had a long talk yesterday with Weston, and after that I had even less pity.

The worst part is that I cannot keep up the pretence, if people

★ Cecil Boyd-Rochfort.

talk to me, that he is a good trainer, and that I only got rid of him on the ground of economy. I shall do it as long as I possibly can, but I know that some day I shall blurt out that he was quite incapable of managing a big English stable. Weston is evidently delighted at the change.

Lambton replied:

We have had twenty articles on the subject written by all sorts of people most of whom are neither gentlemen or good journalists, and God knows what they would write without Galtrey's lead . . . the great difficulty of the situation is the fact that we know, and other people do not, that *we do* want to get rid of Butters and that we want to keep that secret. I hope you will be satisfied with what has been done so far – I have done the best I could, and playing the hypocrite is not a pleasant task, besides that I am most genuinely sorry for Butters – so much so that I at times hate myself for having brought it about – but when I go out to morning exercise as I did this morning I say "thank God".*

Once the dust had settled on the dismissal of Butters, Lord Derby arranged for George Lambton to go to France for a long weekend to inspect and report upon his mares at Madame Couturie's Le Mesnil Stud and his horses in training at Chantilly. His intention was to reduce the number of his mares in France to ten, "but of a better class than those I have already got there". He apologized to Lambton that there would be no room for Cicely at his Paris flat (60 Avenue d'Iéna) as he was allowing the British Ambassador to live there for a month whilst the Embassy was being redecorated, but offered accommodation to his trainer. Subsequently, Lambton wrote:

I had no time in France to write to you. Considering the weather I was very lucky. A fine morning at Chantilly and a fine day at Madame Couturie's. Saint Sauveur told me that they had taken off the night boat from Havre, so I had to come back to Paris. I enjoyed my trip very much and I think everything is very well done at Madame C's Stud; good paddocks; good men on the Stud; the mares and foals look well, and I should say the whole show is A.1., except for the mares themselves, which I have rather a poor opinion of. I am writing you a full report of every

* George Lambton always believed that Butters started giving the horses fast work too soon.

animal. What strikes me is this. As racing is in France today you
have less chance with moderate horses than you have in England, unless you go a long way from Paris. Certainly the com-
petition for the 2 year old races is severe, and there are not so
many opportunities as in England. On the other hand I believe if
you had some fairly good sound staying horses you have a better
chance than in England of making it pay. From what I saw of
your mares, yearlings and foals, I don't think you are at all likely
to breed that class of horse.

Lord Derby was obviously grateful for George Lambton's expert
view, if hardly overjoyed with all his findings:

I am glad you had an interesting time, and I am so glad you found
Le Mesnil a good Stud. I am very fond of Madame Couturie, and
she was so devoted to Victoria and Victoria to her. I should like
therefore to give her something in the way of mares worthy of
the Stud.
    Your report is dismal reading, but I am very glad you have
made it as now I know exactly where I stand. I have got to harden
my heart and clear out practically the lot. I am writing to
Madame Couturie to ask the best way of doing this.
    And now quite a different matter. Will you come out with me
on January 6th to France for a fortnight at Cannes? It is the only
time that I can have you and I shall be so glad if you would come
out as a companion to me. I am going out alone for the first few
days.

A month later Lord Derby, determined upon an economy campaign, made clear his ideas regarding the sale of some of his horses,
and added a postscript reminding George Lambton that Walter
Alston had a strong antipathy to the blood of Tetratema and did not
wish him to be used as a stallion to serve Stanley House mares. "I
think it is as well," he wrote to Lambton, "that I should put down
for you some general instructions with regard to the reduction in
the Stables." He continued:

I wish, as far as I possibly can, to prevent the distress which
looking for new employment must cause to any of the men we
cannot keep on. I can make no promise with regard to pensions
though I shall be ready to consider giving them to any particularly hard cases – such cases must depend entirely on the length
of continuous service they have given to me.

I do not wish any of the men to be out of employment at Christmas time and therefore they will be kept on and paid up to and including the week ending January 10th, but of course if any of them hear of any good place which they want to take before that, please let them go. They will receive a gratuity equal to their pay up to January 10th.

With regard to those who stay, of course there will be no question of any change of wages but with regard to presents on winning there are certain innovations which have crept in of which I had no knowledge and for which I cannot remember having ever given authority. Some years ago a definite scale was laid down by which the boy who did a winner received – I think it was – £1 a £100 in a £1,000 race and under, and after that 10/- a £100, but there never was any question of giving to any of the head lads, the blacksmith, or anybody else, except on special occasions, and for the future any presents that have been made of that description have got to cease.

As a footnote to this letter Lord Derby mentioned that he was sending Lambton an extra present of £500. In his reply Lambton admitted: "It is very welcome as I rather overspent at the Sales and it will come in most useful."

Inevitably the economy campaign necessitated a reduction in the staff at Stanley House, and Lord Derby explained early in December:

I have been into the list of those who have got to be discharged from the Stables, and I find that only Rolfe is really eligible for a pension. With regard to the other men none of them come under the terms of the Knowsley Pension scheme which does not begin to operate till after a man has been with us 20 years. I am however going to pay them as I told you up to January 8th and shall give a small gratuity, probably £1 or so, to each of them when they go.

There is one thing I do want you to look at and that is the number of stablemen who don't ride out. I do think that there are too many of those and when you know exactly how many horses there will be in the Stable next year you may want to make some further readjustment.

Lambton agreed to go to Sansovino:

I will come out on the 6th, although I feel rather a brute leaving my family in the holidays. . . . I only learnt this evening a very disagreeable thing. Owing to this being a Private Stable the men will not get the Dole if they are out of work, and as I hear that 180 stablemen at Newmarket are already out of work the prospects look horrible. I suppose it is correct . . .

Three days later (19 December) he wrote:

I have given notice to 17 men – two of them have the option of taking the places of the loft-man and the stable-cart driver. There are also four apprentices. Two of them Butters takes with him. Unfortunately the other two came into the Stables the year I left and were apprenticed to me. Neither of them are much use, although they are good boys, but they have grown too tall. They are both out of their apprenticeship early next year. I cannot discharge them before their time is up.

. . . the way the men took their dismissal was really quite wonderful. There was only one who grumbled, and most of them expressed their thanks for the good time they had always had at Stanley House, and how sorry they were to go. I knew they were good fellows, but I really was filled with admiration and pity. Most of them are so fond of their horses and their work – and what is before them?

I believe that there is a Committee Meeting over this Limekilns question tomorrow. I should like to tell you something that I think is important and dangerous. I know that Harry Lascelles who is on the Committee is of the opinion that Newmarket would not only be as good without the Limekilns but even better when the new gallops were made. I do not believe that there could be a more mistaken opinion. The Limekilns is the best galloping turf in the world, and has made Newmarket. . . . it does not greatly matter to me as I am so old, but I feel strongly that if you lose the Limekilns that Newmarket is done for.

Three days before Christmas Lord Derby took the opportunity in a letter of seasonal good wishes to write:

Now about the men going. I am very sorry for them all but there it is I cannot help it, circumstances being what they are and if at any time we have vacancies we will try and take any of the old hands back.

With regard to the apprentices, Butters is behaving very badly in taking those two. They may have been apprenticed to him but at the same time they have been paid for by me and it is on my horses that they have had all their practice and I am not sure that if I disputed it at Weatherbys that I should not find, as a matter of fact being a private stable, I could keep them as only being taken on by Butters acting for me. I do not like however to move on this till I know about the dole but I shall certainly treat Butters quite differently now to what I should otherwise have done. . . .

I amused myself last night by taking out 12 mares from our stud list. They have had an aggregate of 66 years at the stud and during these 66 years they have either been barren, slipped foal or had twins 38 times. As the average of twins is supposed to be 1 in 800 it does look to me as if somehow something was wrong, though what it is I can't tell.

The weather in the South of France was glorious, and both Lord Derby and George Lambton were sorry to return to the English winter. Soon after their return they lunched at Claridges, and following their conversation, Lambton wrote to Lord Derby:

I was very much worried when you told me in London that your Racing Stable had cost you so much money last year, and that you had lost on every horse. I could not believe this could be so, unless there was something radically wrong – so I have been very carefully into the stable books and Weatherby's account. I make out that including the salaries and the percentages to Weston and Butters; my salary; Rates and Taxes, repairs, presents and wages to men, that you were considerably on the right side . . . I take some pride in your stables, and if it is run at a loss, I feel that it is a disgrace. . . .

I have been in constant association with Rolfe for 33 years, and no more loyal servant ever lived – I cannot, at his age, let him go to the work-house which I can see no escape from without help. I know you must have a lot of these sort of cases to deal with, and I have no intention of asking you to do anything – and I shall look after him. . . . I am most reluctant to tell you this, as it is the sort of thing that is open to misconstruction, and might look as though I was making myself out as a very good fellow, but I must risk it, and I hope you know me well enough to understand it. In these damnable times you cannot go on as you have been doing, and if I was in your position I should have to do the same but you have not been in daily association with men that have to be turned off when they are old – that makes it more painful and almost impossible to do. That is life and as one gets older oneself the more you come up against it. Last week I had to send away one of the nicest young fellows I ever knew. His father used to be in the stables, now dead, and his mother a really wonderful fighter against adversity. It had to be done, he has no chance of getting work, and these things keep me awake at night. But there is no help for it.

The 1931 season began uneventfully for Lord Derby, and by Ascot he was complaining to George Lambton:

It is rather a dismal outlook for the moment but as you say with patience everything will probably come right . . . We certainly are completely out of luck and I am afraid we must look to a change only when the two year olds come on. I hope that will be by Liverpool and Goodwood.

Lynwood Palmer is taking down 3 pictures, Fairway, Fair Isle and Bosworth, for you to see. I like Fair Isle but with regard to the other two he does not seem quite to have caught the horse. Alice's criticism of Fairway is that his fore-legs look like a bed post, absolutely straight from the ground to the top of the shoulder and also that he has made the joints very coarse. Don't give it to Lynwood Palmer as her criticism but if you agree, give it as yours.

9

Seeds of Doubt

Lord Derby had never had a high regard for Cicely Lambton, due to annoyance that whenever George Lambton was ill she took it upon herself to manage the stables and the Stanley House horses. He believed that her interference in the training of his horses was an impertinence that he could not tolerate, even though he admitted her competence to undertake the task. In the light of this belief an incident at Sandown Park on 17 July 1931 may have been over-emphasized in his mind and sowed seeds of doubt as to his future association with George Lambton and his wife.

His four-year-old Caerleon, a brother of Colorado, had been unplaced in the Victoria Cup and the Kempton Jubilee in the spring, and in midsummer had failed in the Duke of Cambridge Handicap at the Newmarket First July meeting. Yet many people, especially Cicely Lambton, believed that he was a top-class colt, whose potential ability had been highlighted by his starting favourite for the 1930 Two Thousand Guineas (won by Diolite). After the Duke of Cambridge Handicap he contested the Eclipse Stakes, for which no one was surprised that he started at 25–1, for his rivals included such very useful colts as Singapore, Goyescas, Sandwich and Parenthesis. In addition it was realized that the Stanley House fortunes on the Turf were at their nadir, for the racing season was half over and Lord Derby's colours had been successful in only five modest races since March, giving him £1007 – a paltry sum to be credited to the account of an owner who in the previous nine years had headed the Owners List three times and had been in second place in four other years.

Admittedly the Eclipse was run at a false pace, but nevertheless there was general astonishment when Caerleon stormed up the stiff hill to win by two and a half lengths from Goyescas. Lord Derby was present to witness the colt's victory, but left the racecourse soon afterwards, and did not know that later in the afternoon the Stewards – Lord Lonsdale, Sir William Bass and Lt Colonel Giles Loder -- held an Enquiry which was considered a stigma upon the connections of the horse involved. Subsequently they announced that they were satisfied with George Lambton's explanation that Caerleon had been coughing in June, that the colt was a peculiar tempered horse who could not be relied upon, that he had great difficulty in training him, and that since Newmarket, where Weston claimed he ran ungenerously, Caerleon had made rapid improvements.★

However George Lambton was furious – with justification – that in the press the next morning false reports were published that the Stewards had adjourned the Enquiry. He felt that such falsehoods were a serious matter to a man of his reputation as a trainer. Behind the scenes he had suspicions that his wife Cicely had backed Caerleon ante-post to win a considerable sum, for he had not been in the best of health and in consequence had left much of Caerleon's training programme in her undoubtedly capable hands. He was also uncertain as to the extent that Weston was involved in the coup. His one certain thought was that Lord Derby would be mightily displeased at the Stewards' Enquiry, for it implied a slur on the integrity of the stable. To make matters worse, Lord Derby had made it abundantly clear on many occasions that he disliked Lord Lonsdale, and in a letter (20 July) to George Lambton after the Eclipse he wrote:

> The least said the soonest mended over this disagreeable affair. I am sure you are not half as angry as I am but I am glad to see that the whole of the Press takes our side. I am writing a formal complaint to the Stewards of the Jockey Club.
>
> Although one certainly cannot acquit the other two Stewards of blame I am certain that the whole trouble came from Hugh Lonsdale and that both Billy Bass and Giles Loder went away on the Friday evening believing that Hugh was going to tell the Press what the truth was; that the explanation had been accepted and that it would be conveyed to the Press the next day. I am certain that it was a genuine surprise to them when they found that this had not been done. I do not know whether it was malice on the part of Hugh – although I daresay you may have noticed from the very beginning he treated you and me like criminals – or whether, what I believe may be the cause, that his mind is failing.

★ Privately George Lambton thought that Frank Butters had failed to train the horse correctly. He also wished that Carslake had been engaged to ride him at Sandown, for the colt invariably went better for him than for Weston on the gallops. However Lord Derby loyally insisted that Weston rode Caerleon, as he was the stable jockey. If Carslake had been the jockey at Sandown, George Lambton would have felt very confident of victory.

I have been told that before and what little intellect he had has entirely gone.

I should like to have put in the Press that I would not run any horses where he was a Steward but as he makes a hobby of Stewardship that would practically mean not racing at all. As you know for the last 6 or 7 years I have always declined to act as Steward with him and now I see he is a Steward at Liverpool. I am not going to be there this week so it does not matter, but you can find out for me when he was put on as I do not think he was on the list of Stewards at the March meeting.

Now with regard to Caerleon's future,* I have been thinking it over and I am certain that the first thing we ought to do is to strike him out of all handicaps where weights have appeared. You may not agree with me but this I think I must insist on. After that if we put him in a handicap he is handicapped on his last running and nobody can say a word. I am sure when you think it over you will agree with me. If there are any other races that you could put him into – I do not know how the Doncaster Cup would suit him or races of that kind, well and good. Run him also in the Jockey Club Stakes if fit and well and in the Champion Stakes, and meanwhile we can decide whether we send him to the Stud next year or whether we keep him in training for the Ascot Cup.

Once again I do want to tell you how grateful I am to you for the way you have coaxed the horse back into what he now is. I think his winning is the biggest tribute to your skill that you have had in all the years you have trained for me and my father. I am very sorry there should have been all this worry and I freely admit that for part of it I am to blame as I feel now that the right thing would have been for me myself to have asked for an enquiry. I had thought before the race was run that if he did win I would do so but in the excitement of the moment I quite forgot my resolution. I do not know whether Hugh will leap into print but if so please do not answer him. Let me do it.

Lord Derby also was worried about the finances of his racing activities, and admitted (25 August):

---

* Caerleon only ran once more, being unplaced in the Alexandra Stakes at the Doncaster St Leger Meeting before being sent to the Side Hill Stud, Newmarket, at a fee of 48 guineas and one guinea groom's fees. Walter Alston did not want him to go to stud in England and Lord Derby admitted to George Lambton that he might send the colt to stud in France or – to please Alston – keep him in training for another season.

Things have got to such a pitch now that it is quite possible that I may have to close down the Stanley House Stables altogether, and only have such horses in training as can be accommodated at the Sefton Stud. I hope it won't come to this, but at the same time, as you know, things are somewhat alarming and I want to be prepared in case the position arises that I cannot go on training at Stanley House, and could close it and thereby avoid all the rates and taxes, etc.

Days later there appeared the first reference to the foal out of Selene to whom the name Hyperion was given:

You might let me know how the two foals are going on, El Capitan and Selene. They were so small I should think it would be almost best just to break them and then turn them out again. If by any chance you have the same lovely weather that we have probably the sunshine would bring them on a lot. They are both such late foals that they ought to grow considerably.

I do not want this mentioned to anybody. I want to give little Freddy Rickaby a gold watch and I want to put on it the names of his father and grandfather with the names of the first winning horse they rode for me. Can you from any records in the Stable find out what was the first horse on which his grandfather won a race for us. His father I know won his first race on Marchetta and perhaps also from the stable records you could find out what the date is. I think then it would be a nice thing for the boy to have the three dates and the horses engraved on the watch. What do you think?

I badly want a little money at Weatherbys as I am sorry to say the financial state of racing is very bad indeed, and I am very doubtful as to how far I can go on next year.

Lord Derby, like so many other men, was deeply concerned with the economic crises with which Britain was faced at the end of the Twenties, and which led to the fall of the Labour government and the formation of a "National" government which was national only in name.

Lord Derby wrote to Lambton:

It is possible now to realize fairly accurately what economies have resulted from the reduction in the number of horses in training, but of course it is difficult to make a comparison as to the cost of each individual horse as against last year, because the overhead charges remain the same whether the stable is full or half full. It naturally follows that the cost per horse in a stable of 25 is double what it would be in a stable of 50. No doubt there have been great economies, but unfortunately these have been more than coun- ter-balanced by the extra taxation which has fallen on stallion fees, which now fail to meet the total expenses of the whole stable and stud. This year there will be a deficit which will wipe out the reserve which I had.

These are all considerations which I would like you to think over. It might be possible to shut the buildings, take a small stable somewhere else for about 20 horses, and for you to continue to train them, but there would be complications about that which would be difficult to get over.

Three days later (1 September) he wrote again:

I am rather upset, like you, about this fine of Weston's.* The Stewards were a weak lot. Harewood is a very narrow-minded man, and very much guided by what Hugh Lonsdale thinks. Fitzwilliam is a nonentity, and then you come to Hugh, who, we all know, has got a down on Weston. Somebody told me about it the other day – I cannot remember who – and said it dated from last year when Weston stood up to Hugh. Weston is not always very tactful in his manner and apparently Hugh thought he was rude to him. I rather think Walter knows something about it as I think it was at Ayr, and some of his relations may have talked to him about it. Anyhow I put it down to Hugh, and I think the time has come to make a protest, at all events at Liverpool, against his being a Steward. I am therefore thinking of writing to Topham to say that I wish my name taken off the list of Stewards as I cannot serve with Lord Lonsdale, and for the future if he is to be a Steward I shall decline to enter horses. There is no doubt he is half-witted, but it is no reason because he is half-witted he should have this down upon our stable.

Now with regard to Weston. It is all very disconcerting. I ignore everything as regards Hugh Lonsdale, because really he is not competent now to think or act rightly. I doubt that he ever was; but still at the present moment I would not trust him a yard. All the same I have not been happy as you know, for some time with regard to Weston. I think he is honest, but he is certainly

* After an objection in the Park Hill Stakes at Doncaster.

very stupid, and he has given rise to suspicions where none ought to have existed. I will talk the whole thing over with you, but I do not want you to say anything to him yet about a retainer for next year.

I shall talk to you about expenses, but I think I can manage things all right for next year. There is only one change which I am going to make, to which I am sure you will agree, because both you and I benefit from it. You may remember at one time I gave you a free subscription to Swynford and one to Stedfast. Afterwards for purposes of bookkeeping we arranged that instead of your having these two free subscriptions you should pay for them and I should add £500 a year to your salary. That does not work out very well now. In the first place you do not now get two subscriptions to my stallions; and in the second place, when you pay in your £500 I have to pay all the taxes at the rate of 13/6 in the £. So both of us are losers. What I propose therefore for the future is that you should have a free subscription either to Sansovino or Fairway, whichever you may select – you must let Walter know – and one to Bosworth. You get really rather more than at present, and I get considerably more because I do not have to pay on a sum which I have paid to you. I am sure you will see the point of this. . . .

I see in this morning's paper that the Aga Khan has suddenly taken all his horses away from Dick Dawson at a moment's notice.* Do write and tell me what you hear about it. As to my plans, they are very uncertain.

During September Lord Derby prepared a draft of his views on the running costs of Stanley House, which he sent to George Lambton:

Towards the end of the racing year it is possible to estimate fairly accurately what economies have resulted from the reduction in the number of horses in training, and I am sorry to say that the result is not very satisfactory. The reason is not far to seek. It is not that there has been any wasteful expenditure of money, but although the number of horses has been reduced the overhead charges remain the same – the house, salaries, rates and taxes remain the same, whether for 25 horses or for 50, and therefore

---

* This proved to be advantageous to Frank Butters, for the Aga Khan sent him horses to train at Fitzroy House, Newmarket, the stables to which he had moved after leaving Stanley House.

proportionately the cost of the lower number is far higher than the cost of the larger number. This year there is going to be a big deficit, which cannot be made good by the stallion subscriptions, and which will by the end of the year have eaten up the whole of the reserve which I had. I have all the figures prepared to show you.

I feel therefore it is impossible to go on as at present, and I have two alternatives.

(1) To close Stanley House Stables altogether, and send the horses I keep in training to some public trainer or trainers. That of course would be by far the most economical, as one would not have to pay any rates or taxes, and the wages outside would be included in the Five guineas, which I believe is the ordinary charge for a horse.

(2) To lease the Stables to somebody who could bring in other people besides myself and Mrs James. To him, naturally I should send all my horses, paying again the Five guineas a week.

These are the two alternatives, and I have got to make a decision as to which one I adopt. There is one thing however with regard to the second proposition, and that is whether you your-self would care to be the lessee of the Stables. You may be quite sure that I would meet you in every possible way, and we could arrange terms so that the amount of rent you paid to me would be practically nominal, provided I had in return the right to veto any person whom I did not like coming into the Stable, though you may be quite sure I should not be unreasonable; and I am sure with you to choose the people I should never have cause to exercise that right. As you can imagine, it is a most disagreeable thing for me to have to do but I am afraid there is no third alternative.

By the end of October there were rumours that Weston was either ill or had lost his nerve. However Lord Derby's thoughts (31 October) were on holidays:

Now quite another thing. I think it is quite possible as we cannot go abroad that Alice and I and the two children, will come down to Newmarket for a fortnight or so in January. What about membership of the golf club, both at Newmarket and Mil-denhall? Do you think you could put my name down and get me elected for both before the beginning of January as I should want to play at both.

Now one other thing. Suppose the children wanted to hunt

with the Newmarket and Thurlow, is it easy for them to do so? If they met any long distance away we might use the horse van to take their ponies, if it is not being otherwise used. I suppose there is plenty of room down at the farm where we could keep their ponies.

Lord Derby reiterated his concern for Weston's future (5 November 1931):

I really am rather puzzled to know what to do about Weston as I am quite certain he has lost his nerve and I do not suppose at his age he would ever really get it back again, and I think therefore it will be best to leave any question of not riding the horses this year alone, and decide whether or not we will keep him on next year. I believe I give him £1500 a year and at the present moment 10% of the winnings, but I certainly shall knock off the percentage, and I really do not know that he is worth £1,000 a year. However that I would like to talk over with you when I see you next week.

By the spring of 1932 Lord Derby was thinking ahead regarding a successor to George Lambton, who had intimated again during the winter that he was contemplating retirement:

I am afraid it is very doubtful whether I shall get down to Newmarket for the Second Spring and I am obliged to write to you with reference to the future instead of talking it over, as I had meant to, at that meeting.

I feel that with regard to your successor we must not leave any settlement as late as we did last year. As you yourself said, you could only do it for one year and I realize that even that year has been a tremendous tax upon you and it would not be fair to ask you to again shoulder the burden.

I want, however, to carry you with me in choosing your successor. The two I have in mind are Nightingall and Elsey, but the more I think of it with regard to the latter the more I feel that it would not be to his advantage to take him away from the north where he is having a great success. I should therefore propose to see Nightingall and ask him whether at the end of the year he would be ready to take over the Stable. Of course it would be on somewhat different financial lines to the way the Stable has been run in the past, but that would be a question for discussion between him and me.

Just one word of a personal nature. Although this must mean

the severance of your active connection with the training of my horses you may be perfectly certain I shall not forget, in any financial arrangements I make, all you have done for me. I feel to a certain extent it is the passing of the old generation and the beginning of a new one in which I am sure Edward will carry on and I hope with the same success as, thanks to you and Walter, I have had.

I am a bad hand at expressing myself but I think you know how very grateful I am to you for all you have done and for nothing more than for the sacrifice you have made in coming back to undertake the training this year in order to tide me over a very difficult period.

Early in January 1932 Lambton had commented to Lord Derby:

I must say it is very good of you to continue to give me a subscription to Fairway and Caerleon in these hard times – also to pay the whole of Alec Cottrill's salary. It makes a great difference to me . . . have just seen Teddy off to Eton after a day's hunting . . . and more important Hyperion has grown – and in every way is a nice horse. Will come fairly slowly. Goes well. . . . I hope you enjoyed your trip to India. I was lucky at Brighton. Really wonderful weather with a gorgeous sun. With a motor it is quite a good winter resort, and the food is really first class at the Metropole . . .

Lambton fancied Giudecca for the One Thousand Guineas, but the filly disappointed, and a week after the race Lord Derby commented (3 May):

Now with regard to Weston. What he said to you was very extraordinary but I am afraid I am a little more suspicious than you and I am not convinced that he was trying. He was so emphatic to me before the race that The Oaks and not the 1,000 was the race she would win that even before she ran I had a little misgiving about him. I know you always think that The Oaks is more her race than the 1,000 but that is very different. He did exactly what I always object to. He pulled her up in a very marked way. Everybody could see she could certainly have been third without the slightest effort on his part. However I will talk it all over with you when I see you at Kempton.

A month later (9 June) Hyperion, whom George Lambton

considered so perfect in conformation but so small that he would win the Pony Derby at Northolt, was again mentioned – "With regard to the other horses, certainly run Hyperion and Complacent at Ascot, but I am afraid on their trials they cannot have much chance." Despite his owner's lack of optimism, Hyperion won the New Stakes before continuing his career in the Prince of Wales Stakes at Goodwood in July by dead-heating with an unnamed filly sired by Sansovino.

However, Lord Derby still had no conception of the glory that Hyperion was eventually to bring him, and in a letter (20 August) from Gullane, made no reference to him:

> I hope you feel all the better for your brief holiday. I am certainly feeling much better than I did. I am now going to begin a steady course of golf, unless I have to go down to Lancashire, which I do not think is likely, for this strike business; so you can go on writing to me here. If you possibly can, write to me always on the Saturday night with regard to the following week, as otherwise I do not get your letter until the Tuesday morning.

Tommy Weston was still causing consternation, as Lord Derby pointed out on 25 August:

> Really one does not know what to do about Weston. I suppose he has completely lost his nerve at the gate, and when you have the Starter at York and the Starter at Newmarket both reporting the same thing, that he won't go near the tapes, it is quite evident we must make a change. . . . I do not know whether it would do any good to ask the Starters, if it happened again, to formally report him to the Stewards of the Meeting.

In a further letter from Gullane (29 August) he went on to say:

> Just for my own satisfaction I am putting down what my feelings are with regard to Weston, without waiting for your second letter.
>
> To tell you the truth I am not in the least surprised. I always feel myself so ignorant of racing, although I like it, especially about race riding, and I never like to give an opinion as to how a race has been ridden. But there is one thing which has struck me very forcibly, and I think I have mentioned it to you, and that is the number of times our horses have started hot favourites, only to fail. Lately I have been ascribing this to Weston's extraordinary

reluctance to go up to the tapes, and certainly in the case of Complacent and Versicle there seems to have been no question of his stopping them or attempting to stop them once the start was made. But one wonders whether the bad start of both of them, and many others, was in any way intentional.

There can be no doubt in my mind that we cannot continue him as our jockey next year, and whether we should end it now or not is a very difficult matter to decide.

Lord Derby remained at Gullane for much of September. On 1 September he wrote to express his sympathy with Cicely, who was suffering from plant poisoning:

I am sorry for what you tell me about Cicely. My sister-in-law, B. Stanley, who is a great flower expert, is here, and she says plant poisoning is not at all uncommon, but she never heard of it from dahlias before. I hope you are right and that it won't last long as it must be a great bore for her.

I do not particularly want to buy anything at Doncaster but if you saw a nice looking filly who would be an outcross for any of our horses and you could get her for £500 or £600 at Doncaster will you buy her, but please do it in your name. I do not think there is a chance of my coming down. Quite apart from other reasons I do not think it would do for me to go racing while there is this strike on in Lancashire. People would say, "Why does he go racing when he might come here and perhaps be of help to us?" As a matter of fact both sides know I would be ready to help them if I could, but it is no use thinking of intervening when both sides have equally made up their minds they are going to fight to a finish. Personally I think that the operatives would be very glad indeed to see somebody who could intervene and get them such a settlement as would save their faces. There is no doubt whatever, in the opinion of most of them, from what I hear from a man who came up here to see me, their representatives went much further than they were authorised to do, but having gone this far it is very difficult for them now to draw back.

He also commiserated with George Lambton, who had narrowly missed being knocked down by a motorist: "I hope you got the number of the motorist and are going to go for him. The pace at which some motors go through Newmarket is simply disgraceful . . ." He went on to say:

Thanks very much for your two letters received this morning. You will have got my telegram yesterday asking you to put me a pony each way on Udaipur and £10 each way on Fog Horn.

I am incapacitated at the present moment with a bad foot. I personally think it is gout, but contrary to most doctors the doctor here says it is not, and I have only strained my foot. It is extremely painful especially at night, and I cannot get about at all. However I hope it will be well enough for me to go to Doncaster even if I do not go to Lanark.

A month later, at the Newmarket First October meeting, Hyperion was trounced by Manitoba, who finished eight lengths ahead of him in the Boscawen Stakes. Lord Derby's disappointment was obvious and he told George Lambton:

One must not give up hopes of him, but still, although I did not think that he would beat Manitoba, I thought and hoped that he would make a race with him – P.S. Since dictating the above I have got your letter. It gives me hope that the running was quite wrong, and that Hyperion may have been pinched in the shoeing.

As the season drew to its close Lord Derby became more than ever convinced that George Lambton, now seventy-two years old, should resign. However he realized that the subject of the resignation would be no easy matter to broach, much less resolve. He worried about it until he became confused in his own mind as to his best course of action, and then decided that it would be in his own interests to draft a memorandum. In this manner he hoped to consolidate his thoughts:

In speaking to George I think I should begin by telling him that I cannot think that his health would stand another year as Trainer. That I recognize that he only took it on to help me out of a difficulty and that I really do not feel that I can ask him to continue, and that the time to make a break is at a moment when he has had the wonderful success that he has had in training Hyperion. He will never do anything better than that and therefore a fitting moment to end.

I shall say that I cannot help remembering when he originally resigned that Cicely told me that he could not afford to resign, and basing my remarks on that I shall say I hope he will understand that he would not leave me empty handed.

I should then tell him what pension I am ready to give him. I have not quite decided that yet.

I should say then that this time I could not think of retaining him as a Manager. It was not successful last time and I would not therefore entertain the idea of repeating the experiment for one moment.

I shall point out to him that what I am doing is in the interests of both of us. That I do not feel he is strong enough or well enough to do it and I really will not go through next year as I have gone through this year with the repeated breaks in training.

If George, after I have talked to him, still sticks to it that he can perfectly go on training, it will be very difficult for me to say, "I won't have you." It is equivalent to actually dismissing him which naturally I do not want to do, but if he insists on going on he will probably say that he will find somebody to do some of the donkey work and that he can do a great deal through Cicely and Teddy.

I shall then have to take a different line and say, "Very well, if you think you can do it, go on, but you must remember if there is a breakdown in your health next year, which will put both you and me in a hole, I shall not promise that I will renew the offer I now make, but if you do go on there must be certain conditions. When you were ill last year I made some enquiries as to whether I could get somebody to do the work under you, and I must tell you perfectly straight that although I might have found one or two who would, I was told on very good authority that nobody would accept the position as long as Cicely had the influence in the Stable she had and gave the orders which she did do, nominally through you, though there is no doubt in the summer she took an authority with regard to the Stables which personally I resented at the time. I did not say or do anything about it because I knew you were ill and did not want to worry you any further, but there is no doubt the Stable was very unhappy generally during the weeks you were away and poor Alec Cottrill especially so. I must therefore, if you go on, make it a definite rule that Osgood is your deputy. That no orders whatsoever are given in the Stable, or to jockeys, except by you direct or if you are not well enough to do it then by an instruction in writing signed by yourself."

I shall say I am very sorry to have to say this but I really will not stand what went on this summer.

Curiously, having drafted this memorandum, Lord Derby seemed to allow the subject to be held in abeyance instead of taking positive action.

In February 1933, Lambton wrote to Lord Derby, who was at Sansovino:

> Hyperion, Highlander and Scarlet Tiger are all doing really well so far – I see that the touts mistook Hyperion for Highlander, as they said that Hyperion had finished on the heels of Serbus with Highlander behind. It was the other way about. Blackwell* came round stables last night. He liked all three horses but thought Hyperion looked the fittest. He is right.

By the end of March Lord Derby was hopeful that a successful season lay ahead:

> I had to rush away – and, by the way we only just caught the train – so did not have time to talk with you about the Rickaby retainer. I shall be very glad to have the boy and would give him a retainer of £500 a year. If other members of the Stable made use of him then I should expect them to pay a small share. I hope you will make it right with Weston that he shall not think we were taking on a boy very nearly his own weight to displace him. Say it is only really out of affection for the Rickaby family who have served us for 3 generations and really it is only replacing Wells, to whom, as I told you I would give no retainer.
>
> It is splendid your beginning so well and I hope that Dorigen's† success will be followed by a good many more. I cannot help having great hopes of Thrapston. . . .
>
> Highlander we could perhaps decide about when I get down there tomorrow. I do not think after his running the other day‡ we can run him. It would create a tremendous talk if he made anything like a race with the winner. That is entirely owing to Weston's bad riding. I know he did not want him to run in the 2,000 because I suppose he wanted to ride another horse and I cannot help wondering whether he did not allow himself deliberately to be shut in so that the horse should not make a show.
>
> Now with regard to Thursday I shall not be there and I would do just what you like about Hyperion, but my own idea would be

---

* George Blackwell, the venerable trainer who won the 1903 Triple Crown with Rock Sand.

† Winner of the Lincoln, trained and owned by George Lambton and ridden by Tommy Weston.

‡ Unplaced in the Free Handicap at the Newmarket Craven Meeting.

to run him in the Chester Vase. It is a good race to win and I like winning up there.

Hyperion duly won the Chester Vase, and a delighted Lord Derby commented:

> It was indeed good news about Hyperion and the papers confirm what you said in your telegram how very lazily he ran. Still it is a good thing to have him show his best form when out.
>
> By the way I cannot remember whether I asked you which I certainly do now – to be my guest at the "Derby Club" Dinner on Thursday May 25th. I will let you know about the place and time later. It ought to be rather amusing. It is a new Club, 100 strong and we have a selling sweep after dinner. We are following on the lines of the old "H.B." Club who used to ask some bookmakers.
>
> The Prince of Wales is coming as my guest and I want you to come too.

It seemed that George Lambton might saddle three runners for The Derby – Hyperion, his pacemaker Thrapston, and Scarlet Tiger, owned by his brother, Lord Durham. Inevitably there were complications regarding the jockeys, and these were aggravated by Lambton's illness. He did not feel well enough to write a letter, so that on 25 May Cicely told Lord Derby:

> George has asked me to write to you tonight and say the horses are quite all right . . . Carslake won't be able to ride Thrapston as he has promised if Highlander did not run to ride Statesman. I believe that there is a possible chance of getting Donoghue and Joe Childs is supposed to have no ride, but George thinks that the latter is not at his best at Epsom nowadays . . . George was very seedy on Monday and Tuesday with a bad go of muscular rheumatism but this is getting better and I am pleased with him tonight. He has been much more comfortable all day. I am afraid that there is no possible chance of his getting to Epsom while he is in this state and there is a lot in the *Evening Standard* about George in a bath-chair. Not a word of truth in it – I wish there were!

The 1933 Derby proved a marvellous victory for Hyperion, ridden by Tommy Weston, who beat King Salmon by four lengths. Thrapston, the pacemaker for Hyperion, and ridden by Donoghue, finished fifth. George Lambton listened to the BBC race commentary on the radio, but a supremely happy Lord Derby was at Epsom to greet his hero after his spectacular triumph.

The day after The Derby, Hyperion's owner wrote congratulating his trainer:

> I am sending you a dictated and typewritten letter as I have to go to this India Committee and then shall go down for a couple of races to Epsom, as I want to see Donoghue – I wasn't able to do so yesterday – and thank him. But even if I had hours I could not find words enough to thank you for what you have done with Hyperion. Nobody but you could have brought him to the post in the state he was in – perfectly trained. He would not have blown a candle out and there is no doubt he is a smashing good horse.

A month later Hyperion, who had added to his Derby victory by winning the Prince of Wales Stakes at Royal Ascot, was causing concern, and Lord Derby wrote (10 July) to George Lambton, who had just returned from Bagnoles-de-l'Orne:

> I expect you have been rather worried, as I was, about Hyperion, but Reynolds saw Alice at Haydock and gave her a very reassuring account and I talked to him and Osgood on the telephone yesterday and equally got a good account, so I hope it may prove to be nothing, but it must give us some cause for anxiety.
>
> Another reason why it causes anxiety is that we have had such a lot of this stifle trouble. Reynolds told Alice far and away beyond the average of other stables. He told her he was sure it was not due to the boxes and as far as he could see it was not hereditary as Venetia's animals have had it as much as ours. I wonder if it has anything to do with the private gallop – that longer gallop with a rather sharp bend on a slope?

The following week he was even more perturbed:

> I am terribly disturbed at your message with regard to Hyperion. Though one hopes he may not put out his stifle again still I am afraid it wipes out any chance of his being really fit for the Leger, and one would not run him unless he was absolutely fit. We shall have to hope that either Highlander or Thrapston will be able to take his place. I have not got the book with me. I think they are both still in.
>
> I should make no attempt to hide it. Let the public know that he

has done this, and it is very doubtful if he can be prepared for the race.

Seventy-two-year-old Walter Alston died at the end of July, with one obituary notice stating: "In the mating problems which constantly confront breeders he was a slave to no abstract theory. The lexicon that he used was common sense based upon solid facts. And the outcome was the splendid array of breeding stock in Lord Derby's Stanley House stud, the like of which has no equal in any breeding establishment in the world." It pleased Lord Derby and also George Lambton that he had lived long enough to know of Hyperion's Derby victory.

George Lambton wrote in *Scapa Flow – A Great Brood Mare*, printed privately in 1937:

During the latter years of his life Walter Alston was a martyr to asthma, and lived very quietly at Falmouth Cottage, Newmarket, surrounded by his Stud Books and other racing literature, but he was also a voracious reader. There was no good book or memoir that did not find its way into his library, and this enabled him to escape the one track mind so often characteristic of a man living much alone. No one knew more about the Stud Book and pedigrees, and he was a man of strong opinions and often strong prejudices, but, like all clever men, he was never satisfied with what he knew and always wanted to know more. His life was with his mares, foals and yearlings. His paddocks were beautifully kept, his stud men were devoted to him and well-trained; no wonder that he made a success of the job to which he gave his life.

As the day of the St Leger approached, Lord Derby was worried about his own health:

The doctor tells me that my foot is a little better today, but I cannot say that I feel that it is. He seems doubtful whether I shall be able to get to Doncaster, but personally I have no doubts that I intend to come, although I expect it will mean staying in the Box most of the time.

My foot is much better but still not right, and I shall have to wait till Monday before I know really whether I can go racing. If it was gout pure and simple I should know whether or not I could come, but with this phlebitis one has to be very careful it does not spread up the leg, as it looked like doing yesterday.

I can quite understand what you say about Hyperion. We can

only hope for the best and pray for a little rain, but at the present moment as far as this place is concerned it does not look like there being any change. It is bad luck for me. A lovely time like this, having to stay in the house with my leg up the whole week; and what with the leg and racing I shall not be able to golf next week – and I was rather pleased with my golf this year.

Hyperion, again ridden by Weston, won the St Leger from Felicitation and Scarlet Tiger, but he did not race again during 1933 and Lambton wrote:

We had some trouble with Hyperion last week which I did not worry you with at the time as the trouble would probably be over in two or three days, and it would cause you anxiety for nothing. Everything is now all right. On Wednesday he came out of the stable very short, and a lot of heat in his feet. Osgood sent for Reynolds, it was an attack of laminitis but not acute. He was much the same Thursday morning, but from that moment it began to subside, and he is now all right. The cause of the attack was probably from two things, first that curious attack he had in the box coming to Doncaster there must have been something to cause that. It was almost impossible that it could have been ordinary indigestion, it was more likely to be some poisonous matter which got into the passage of his bowels. (I am not hinting at foul play); but this is Reynolds' opinion. The bowels would pass it away, but not quite out of the system; then the gallop on that very hard ground to drive it to the feet. I should say that this is probably the right explanation but I do not think that he should race again this season, even before this trouble I had my doubts. To get him fit for the St Leger I had in some ways to be very hard on him. First of all this stifle trouble, and then his working so lazily at home, he was quite a fortnight behind time and after his gallop* at Lambourn I had to give him two heavy sweats. I should say that there is no doubt that the foot trouble was coming on when he ran. Weston told me this evening that he went down so badly in the canter that he thought we were beaten before we started. Well that is all over, and I think if you don't run him again, you will have a champion next year. On reading my letter again it may look as if Reynolds suspects foul play. That is not the case at all. It was one of those things that can happen to any horse, or any human being.

* Lambton usually spelt the word "galop".

In retrospect George Lambton never thought Hyperion to be the equal of Swynford, and privately would say: "Swynford was the best horse that I ever trained. I knew what Hyperion could do, but I never knew what Swynford could not do. He could beat any horse from 5 furlongs to 5 miles." As against this, Lord Derby thought that Fairway was the best horse ever to have carried his colours.

10

Acrimony and Anguish

Despite the immense success with Hyperion throughout the year, Lord Derby decided in November 1933 that the moment had finally come to terminate his long association with George Lambton as his trainer. For more than thirty years they had shared a belief that all others should be considered as individuals in their own right, irrespective of class or creed; had hated any form of injustice; tended to support the "underdog"; and had been sufficiently gullible to be taken in by hard-luck stories. In addition they had both detested excess, particularly gluttony, drunkenness and vulgarity. Yet perhaps the similarity of their outlook had ended there, although they both put the implications of the word "Duty" high on their list of priorities.

George Lambton, with an innate authority which was seldom questioned by those who worked for him, had always been more radical by temperament than Lord Derby, and without question the more decisive in his actions. He had never suffered fools gladly; loathed "humbug"; was scrupulously honest; and refused to recognize any justification in the nickname "Genial Judas" given to Lord Derby, for he believed the accusation that the Earl was devious to be totally unfair. However he had always remained unconvinced that the benign and affable Lord Derby would abide by his first decision on almost any subject. This lack of conviction was founded on his realization that Lord Derby could be impetuous, and that he would write and post a letter and then send a telegram beseeching the recipient not to open it.

Lord Derby's decision to end George Lambton's position as his private trainer was not, however, made on the spur of the moment. He had been mulling over the situation for some time, as the memorandum prepared in 1932 proved, and was becoming increasingly bemused as to the best decision to make upon what he considered to be a miserable state of affairs. One factor which influenced his judgement was his obdurate belief that when George Lambton was unwell Cicely continued to manage the stables. He did not question her competence, and her experience was second to none, but he could never discard the nagging doubt that there was a distinct possibility that she might attempt to bring off one or more further "coups" with his horses, thus bringing the Stanley reputation into disrepute. Such a thought was reprehensible.

Ironically, matters came to a head after George Lambton had been at Bagnoles in Normandy. Staying in the same house-party was a lady who was a mutual friend of both men. Misguidedly she wrote to Lord Derby implying that George was ill and had told her that he would like to give up training. Inadvertently her letter started the fuse which made Lord Derby feel obliged to write to George Lambton. It was no easy letter to compose, and several drafts were prepared before he believed he had struck the correct note:

I had particularly hoped to talk over something with you if you had been well enough to come up to Knowsley last week or to London this week, then I should not have had to put in writing what I have to do now, as it is always much easier to express one's thoughts and for them to be understood when talking matters over than when writing. I should then not have had to put in words the horrible fact that faces me, that it is only at the complete sacrifice of your health that you can go on training, and I am not selfish enough to ask for that. Your skill has been backed up by your pluck and enthusiasm during the last six months when you have in the training of Hyperion had the biggest triumph of your always successful career. But to continue at that pressure would be too great a sacrifice to yourself. While you and I must feel the sadness of making the break which means parting with the best trainer anybody has had, and one whose triumphs have made my horses known all over the world, neither of us can go back to our youth. I am not a good hand at expressing myself as I should like to do, but I do want you to understand that I recognize what a deep debt of gratitude I owe you, and one cannot end a racing connection of forty years without many heartfelt regrets. But I hope you will recognize the motives which make me end it now and that this friendship of ours, unbroken for forty years will continue to the end.

One does not like at a moment such as this bringing in the financial question, but it is only fair to mention that I hope you will allow me to give you for the first six months of next year your present salary, that is to say £1000 and after that for your life an allowance of £1200 a year to compensate you for giving up training and as repaying part of the debt of gratitude for all you have done for me.

George Lambton replied:

> Although I was told in July when I returned from Bagnoles that you had approached another trainer about taking your horses I brushed it aside as idle gossip and our interview yesterday came as a complete and utter surprise to me, in fact the blow had to take its time to sink in before I realized the force of it. Of course you have every right to make what arrangements you like regarding the training of your horses but you had no right to do what you have done in such a way. After forty years' service you dismiss me with six weeks' notice. Surely this must be a record! All this autumn when I have been with you, talking of the yearlings and planning their entries you have known in your heart that I was to have nothing to do with them, in fact you accept my services up to the last moment and when there is nothing more to be done the knife falls!
>
> You will remember that when you parted with Butters I insisted that he should be told when the yearlings came up, so as to enable him to make arrangements. Now as to the future, although by keeping this matter secret you have made it increasingly difficult for me, I have no intention of giving up training and as soon as I can arrange matters I shall start myself. There is one thing I should like to know, what is Osgood's position? I shall have to tell him directly I go home that I am leaving. Does he remain in the stable or has he to look for another situation?
>
> I am here till this evening.

Tragically, this correspondence caused a rift to appear in their friendship, and both were becoming obstinate, with their intentions being so firmly expressed that neither could yield an inch, or give any ground as a concession to the other. Lord Derby wrote (22 November):

> The enclosed is a more or less formal answer to your letter. I should be telling you less than the truth if I did not tell you how hurt I am that an offer of mine made in all sincerity in the hopes that it would for the rest of your life relieve you both of work and of financial anxiety should be received in the way you have received my offer. I had the hopes that it would be welcomed by you and prevent any break in our friendship, even if it did end our racing association. For the moment I feel I have failed and yet I

cannot help hoping that on further consideration you will see my point of view and appreciate my offer in the spirit in which it was offered.

The "enclosed" elaborated the original letter:

You may not believe that it hurt me very much indeed to say what I did to you yesterday but it has hurt me much more to receive your letter this morning in which I think you do me far less than justice.

I am not going to enter into any argument with you but there are certain things which I am unable to allow to pass unnoticed.

First with regard to the suddenness of the blow. I must take you back some time. When you took over again from Butters, and I shall never be grateful enough to you for what you did on that occasion, you distinctly said that you could only do it for a year or two at the outside. You had previously resigned on the ground that your health would not stand training. Is it therefore to be wondered at, 6 years later, when you wrote to me as you did in the summer to say you feared you might be crocked for good, that I should look about to see whom I could find to replace you. I made no secret of having enquired whether one or two people, one man in particular, would be prepared to exercise supervision over the Stable during your absence and if that was prolonged perhaps take it over permanently. However, no further step at the moment was necessary and I had hoped that your then illness would be a passing one. But as a matter of fact what with another accident and another illness I had to contemplate the fact that it was necessary for me to make a permanent change. I did not do this, as I told you, without very great consideration but before the Liverpool Meeting this year had definitely come to the conclusion that the change would have to be made and if you had been able to come to Knowsley I had meant to tell you then. You were not able to come and I had, through your illness and from no fault of my own, to delay speaking to you till yesterday. I could it is true have written, and if you had not been able to come yesterday I should have written, but I preferred to talk to you in the hopes that you would realize that what I was doing was perhaps more in your interests than in my own, because as I can honestly say I can never get any trainer equal to yourself.

Now to come to the second point. You say that "after 40 years' service to dismiss me with 6 weeks' notice. Surely this must be a record." Nobody recognizes more than I do what that 40 years record has meant to me but that I dismiss you with 6 weeks' notice is really a most unfair way of putting the situation and I must insist on your considering the second part of my offer which is that after 6 months is over I was prepared to give you a permanent pension of £1,200 a year for the rest of your life. I did that in the hopes that I should be giving you enough to prevent your having to continue that strenuous work as trainer which in my opinion means a strain on you which you cannot stand. Your construction therefore to my mind is most unfair to me.

You talk of my having allowed you to make all the entries for next year without telling you that you would have nothing to do with the training of the horses entered. Again I must say this is not fair. In the ordinary course of your engagement with me you would have done this and as long as you were so engaged so long did I consider I had a right to ask you to do the duties which belonged to it. You quote the example of Butters and how you brought Butters in but may I point out to you that that is not a fair analogy. You were going to remain as Manager and therefore naturally wished to act in conjunction with Butters, surely a very different situation from the present one.

Now with regard to your statement that owing to my having kept it secret so long it deprives you of the chance of continuing as trainer. I think you know me well enough to know that I would not let the question of money interfere in any way to the detriment of the goodwill between you and me. I am prepared to recognize that 6 months' notice may seem too short and I shall most certainly pay you the full salary for a year from the 1st of January. That I think should obviate any financial criticism that you can make.

I had never approached any other trainer to take over the horses except the two whom you knew I had approached some years ago – Cecil Rochfort and Nightingall. I have naturally considered whom I should ask to take your place and my choice for good or ill has fallen upon C. Leader. I had never spoken to him before I talked to you yesterday. Indeed I did not know him even by sight but after yesterday's conversation I did approach him and find that he will be willing, on certain conditions, to take over the training of the horses, and here I can answer the one question you put to me as to what is to happen to Osgood. I spoke to Leader and asked him whether he would be prepared to keep him on. He said he would with the best will in the world and very glad to do so. It will be up to Osgood to say whether or not he is ready to accept the position, but if you are speaking to him you can say that I place great store on his remaining where he is. That he will be in exactly the same position as he was in regard to you, with the same house and with the same salary. In regard to all the others that will be for Leader to make his own selection. I hope most of them will remain but naturally I would not impose upon him, any more than I did upon you, the necessity of keeping any one particular person.

In order to avoid a possible misunderstanding there is another matter which I must tell you. In the summer Mrs James spoke to me as to the possibility or the reverse of your continuing training and asked me whether I contemplated a change. I told her that at the moment I was only considering whether I should get somebody in to supervise during your illness but that if later in the year I felt I had to make a change she should be the first person that I told. As a matter of fact, as I told you before, I had meant to speak to you at Liverpool and not one further word did I say to her on the subject till after that meeting. I then felt, when I had made up my mind (and it was only then that I did make up my mind), it was only right to tell her especially as she had written again to ask what my decision in the matter was. I went to see her. I told her what I proposed to do and I told her, as I tell you, that I really believed I was acting in your best interests and certainly not in my own, and she told me then, and has since confirmed it in a letter, that she wished her horses to remain at Stanley House, and moreover gave me authority to act for her. Needless to say the last thing I should like would be to leave you under the impression that I had tried to get her horses away from you, though at the moment I did not know you would be going on training. I shall not for the moment act on her letter. I would ask you therefore to continue doing for her what you have done up to the present. I shall communicate with her in India by telegram. Tell her what has happened and leave it to her to decide what she wishes to do. . . .

With regard to entries for myself I gather that it would be repugnant to you to continue making those which will close on December 4th. If that is so perhaps you would let me know in order that I may give authority to Leader to act for me.

Lady Derby felt that she too must write to George Lambton, who answered her letter on November 25th:

My dear Lady Alice,
I must thank you for your very nice letter, and I know what you say comes from the bottom of your heart. You have been much in

my thoughts during this most distressing week, and I know that the position of myself and Eddie must have given you unhappiness and worry, almost as great as it has caused me. There are positions where you have to fight for your life and this is one; it would have been easy for me to say to Eddie, thank you very much and swallow the gilded pill, and to be put quietly on the shelf, and perhaps if the way had been prepared and some persuasion used, I might have been weak enough to succumb. But without one word either to me or Cicely, my whole interest in life was shut down in five minutes. In your letter you write "so many people, who know you have said that you felt you could not go on with the hard work of training". I have never said such a thing in my life to anyone, and it has been very far from my thoughts. It is true that in the first fortnight after my accident before The Derby I was very doubtful if I should ever be any good again. But since then I have got better and better. Will you tell me who are the people who said that I thought I could not go on? All my friends including Eddie knew that I took Teddy away from School in order that he might be with me in the last few years I trained and in face of much adverse criticism. That is in itself proof positive that I had no thought of retiring.

It seems so useless writing, the same thoughts keep coming back and back again, why did not Eddie come to me, his old friend, why did he go to Venetia and tell her his plans, without a word to me, who has managed, trained and bred her horses for years. I can find no answer. I think it has nearly broken my heart. I was so looking forward to next year. I can say no more, except that my affection for you will always be the same.

Lady Derby thought that his letter required a reply:

Just to thank you for your letter and your understanding of my feelings for you.

I expect I employed the term "*so many people* knew etc" rather loosely in the way that you say "all my friends knew that I took Teddy away from school to be with me, etc" – I for one friend had not the faintest idea why you took him from Eton except that you told me at luncheon at Mougins that he was coming away because they taught him everything there – that he would live at home to learn everything that was useful for anyone having to do with horses as I consider that the parents are the only proper judges for what is right for their children I never enquired any further. About the gilded pills? Its origin was not as you think when you were so seedy after your accident and again after Doncaster, Eddie was convinced that you would be coming to him to say you were not strong enough to stand such a strenuous life of training a big stable of horses; I also felt that this was going to happen and you know I don't jump to conclusions as a rule.

In order that you should have no anxiety about your life of leisure and only occupation you created for yourself – the pill was thought of and was meant to be in the nature of *pick-me-up*. However things did not turn out like this. If only one could see the working of other peoples minds – we would have seen how really well and strong you felt and you would have seen how Eddie's action had been worked up to. Alas! that so much success and pleasure should end like this.

You know perfectly well that he could not want any one but you to train for him – you who are a better trainer when you are ill than others when they are well – you accuse Eddie of going behind your back – but he was only preparing himself for the blow that he expected to fall on him, when you might say you must resign after the year of bad health and accidents that you have suffered from. I who am with him from day to day know how worried and unhappy he has been – and you being of the same age as he is must realize that people are not the same as in their youth – have a more nervous way of doing things and that between people in or near the seventies more misunderstandings arise than they do in early life – I do think it a pity that things should come to this pass. You naturally feel you are right in writing and speaking as you do – but I still hope that you may see the other side of the question – please don't answer this, unless it is to say (at some time) that you are understanding.

Edward Stanley also wrote to George Lambton:

My father told me yesterday of his interview with you and I would have written at once but had to go up to Lancashire.

You have been so kind to me and I have been so fond of you when I was a boy that it makes the present position here beastly and this letter harder to write.

I was very sorry to read your *Statement* last night – but still hope that you will take a kinder view of my father's proposal. There can be no question of lack of skill – you have made the most wonderful come back in the History of Racing, but there is one thing over which one has no control and that is health – and my father's proposal was made in the fear that the strain of another year's training would be too much for you and in the hope that you would be able to enjoy some well earned leisure. Retirement, though it must come some time, is always a wrench but I do hope that you will be able to realize that my father's motives were not so unkind as you appear to think now.

Whatever the future may be, I shall always be grateful to you for giving me an enjoyment in racing far greater than I could have otherwise had.

Lambton replied:

My dear Edward,
I got your letter this evening. It is hardly necessary for me to say that this week has been a very distressing one for me, not only for the possible break-up of my life, but for the probable break-up of very old and dear associations. You will probably have seen my letters to your father. I had no complaint to make if you wished to change your trainer, but I have every reasonable complaint to make that I was not told at an earlier date. I don't understand all this stuff about my ill-health. I had a very severe accident this summer and another one later on the same leg, but when you were staying with me for the 1st October Meeting was there any evidence that I was unable to attend to my duties? Perhaps you found it so but I was not aware of it. Anyhow the physician generally asks the patient how he is feeling, and there has never been one word from you or your father to ask me whether I was feeling the strain too great! And I gather that is the reason for my dismissal. Perhaps what has hurt me as much as anything is this, I have managed, bred, and trained Venetia James' horses since Arthur died, I get this telegram from her to say, "Sorry cannot cancel arrangements made before leaving with Derby." So it is evident that your father went behind my back and without one word to me took away the one person that I had every right to count upon. Such a disloyal action I cannot forgive.

Meanwhile Lord Derby was writing to George Lambton's brother:

My dear Durham,
I had intended writing to you before the news became public that I have decided to make a change in my training arrangements and George will cease to train for me at the end of this year. You may

rest assured I have only done this after most careful consideration and the change is solely due to the fact that in my opinion George's health does not warrant his continuing. I am sorry to say he has taken my decision very hard. I told him yesterday – it is in the Press today – hence my apparent discourtesy in not informing you.

I had hoped that the pension I proposed to give him (£2,000 a year for the first year and £1,200 a year after that for life) would have enabled him to give up training but that is not so, and he means to continue on his own.

I have appointed C. Leader to train for me in the future. With regard to your horses naturally I should be very pleased if you kept on with me but equally naturally you may wish to go with George and I would not for the world allow it to be supposed I had advised you to the contrary.

I hope Osgood and others will stay on and everything will be the same except that the charge will be £4.10/- a week instead of £5. I am taking some extra charges on my own shoulders.

I am very much upset at this unfriendly – on his part – break with George but I really had no alternative after his constantly recurring illnesses which left the stable for weeks without a head.

From Alnwick Castle came a letter from Lord Durham to Lord Derby:

Thank you for your very nice letter. We have been moving about lately and it has taken some days to find me. After all these years of closest association and friendship I can well understand how distressing it must be for you to see the turn affairs have taken. With regard to my horses now at Stanley House, George hoped I would let him have them and I said "Yes" to that – in the circumstances I could not see that there was anything else to do. I would like to take this opportunity of thanking you for your kindness in having let me keep my horses in your delightful stable – and of wishing you the best of luck for the coming season.

Whilst George Lambton sent a further letter to Lord Derby:

My dear Eddie,
When I wrote that you only gave me six weeks' notice I was not referring to the financial side of the question, but to my Life's work. Up to the time that I went into your room at Derby House on Sunday, neither by word or deed had either you or Edward

given me the slightest hint that you were about to terminate my engagement although I had been in constant communication with you during the last two months. In five minutes time you told me that on the first of the year I should no longer be your trainer. I think it was the greatest shock I ever had in my life – that is what I meant by "6 weeks' notice for 40 years' work". You and I have been friends for many years; we have had good times together. You have done innumerable kindnesses to me which I will always remember. I know your greatest qualities; your generous nature and affection for your friends; I also know your weakness. I doubt if it is possible for any man to know another better than I know you. In this instance I say that you have let your weakness control your better qualities. If you had straight-forwardly and candidly told me at the proper time what your intentions were, none of this trouble would have arisen, I should have been well out of your way, and have started a fresh life for myself – as it is now it is almost impossible to get anything started before the winter sets in – for the present about the horses, the sooner Col. Leader takes over, especially the yearlings, the better, so far as the entries are concerned any help that I can give him will be most gladly given. He is a very old friend of mine. There is nothing repugnant to me in doing this. What was repugnant to me was that I should have been in constant companionship with you and Edward in this connection, and that you hid from me such a very vital step in my life.

George Lambton wrote to his brother, who had attempted to console him:

Many thanks for your letter. I wish I had seen you. As you may imagine this affair has been a very great grief and worry to me, not only for the complete break up of my life but for the break up of old and happy associations.

It is all very well for Eddie to make protestations of goodwill and his sorrow at hurting my feelings, what did he expect my feelings to be when without a word of warning he closes down my life work, my interest in life, my livelihood with five weeks' notice. It is impossible that anyone can believe that he did not know that I was looking forward with every anticipation to training Hyperion and his extra good lot of yearlings next year. That he was afraid that I would not be capable of doing justice to his horses is now evident not only from his action, but from what he has said to other people. There was only one person for him to have consulted as to my health and that was myself.

In forty years I have given him no reason to suppose that I would undertake a job that I could not perform. Any man may have a bad accident but that does not mean ill health. But what has really hurt and disgusted me is the secrecy that Eddie worked with an old friend without giving him a chance to say one word. . . .

By the end of the month there could be no denying the acrimony which prevailed, and Lord Derby told George Lambton:

I only got back to London early this morning to find your letter. I wish I thought that letters passing between us improved the position but I can only hope that what I now write to you may contribute to a better understanding on your part of my position.

You say my "weakness" controlled my better feelings. This "weakness" consisted in trying to find the most kindly way of placing the situation before you. If that attitude on my part is not so accepted, well and good, it must remain your opinion. It certainly is not mine.

You suggest looking back. It might have been better perhaps for me to have said two months ago what I said the other day and if I had been able to come racing at Newmarket as much as usual I might have done it – I cannot say – but would the position have been improved? Your attitude would have probably been the same and what would have been our position vis a vis each other for the last two months with you in the frame of mind you now are. Surely too from the financial side, to put it on the lowest ground, it was kinder to you, instead of giving you 2 or 3 months' notice, to give you instead, as I now do, full salary of £2,000 for next year, an offer which still holds good.

There was another reason however which does not seem to have suggested itself to you. For many weeks this year the Stable, for reasons which I deplore, has been left without a head. The man whom you yourself had chosen, Alec Cottrill, to help you, you said had failed you. I admit you told me that in the summer but I hope you will equally admit that it would have been far too hard on the boy to have got rid of him in the middle of the racing season.

To continue, I had thought, and kept on thinking, that you would have made some sort of gesture yourself and suggested a discussion of the question of the future but no offer came from you and it was only when I felt that none was forthcoming that I told you of my decision. Is it so very surprising with the knowledge of your frequent absences this year I should have thought that your health was not strong enough to stand the very strenuous work of managing a big stable when 7 years ago you resigned from the post of trainer on the ground that your health would not stand the strain. One does not grow younger in 7 years and the total amount of your absences from active training operations this year surely was ample reason for me to suggest your giving up the work which you found too strenuous 7 years ago.

Believing and hoping that you might approach me with some suggestion for the future management of the Stable and none being forthcoming, I felt that perhaps the reason why you did not do so was the financial one and I therefore made a proposal to you which you have rejected (and which naturally falls to the ground), that if you did give up training I would undertake to pay you £1,200 a year for your life. I confess that when I made it to you, and this is perhaps also one of the reasons why I did not speak to you earlier, it never crossed my mind for one minute that you would reject the offer. You may not believe it but I want again to assure you that I made the offer in the firm belief that you would accept it with a feeling of relief. Instead of that you wrote me a letter the tenor of which I greatly resent and further made communication to the Press from which it would appear that I had dismissed you, as you yourself said in your letter to me at six weeks' notice and with no indication that such notice was coupled with proposals which I do not think the outside world could think ungenerous.

With regard to a further communication you made to the Press dealing with an answer which I gave to a direct question as to what the cause of dismissal was, I may say at once that I gave the question of health because it was the real one and was not any of the reasons which apparently rumour was attributing to our break. I certainly did not do so with any intention of damaging you at the outset of your new venture.

One further point. I made you an offer with regard to stallion fees. I quite realize to withdraw that offer now when you have presumably made arrangements for the matings of your mares next year might place you in a difficulty and I want you to understand therefore that for the season 1934 it still holds good.

I have today signed the authority for Leader to act and he will make the necessary engagements due on December 5th and December 12th.

Osgood is coming to see me on Monday to tell me his decision as to whether he remains with me or not. I shall be very sorry if he leaves me but at the same time I shall quite understand if out of loyalty to you with whom he has been so long associated he prefers to leave.

George Lambton replied, mentioning the financial aspects of their break:

My dear Eddie,
I understand from Lloyd that you are prepared to offer me £2,000 for next year and then £1,200 a year for my life. As it has always been between us, your financial arrangements for me have been generous and always accepted by me with gratitude and pleasure, and I am quite prepared to accept your proposition if you could add this. In the event of my death before December 31, 1939, that sum should be paid to my wife if living, or in the event of her death, to be divided between my two children Edward and Sibyl. It is idle to pretend that at this moment my feeling towards you is the same as before, but I have no wish to embarrass you or your family in any way now or in the future. Time softens many things and I live in hope of that.
Yours, George Lambton.
P.S. I should like to make one thing clear. Lloyd met you yesterday not as my legal adviser but as a mediator.

Mr Lloyd had previously written to Francis Ellis, a legal adviser at Knowsley:

Mr Lambton has consulted me about his disagreement with Lord Derby and has shown me the correspondence. He is extremely upset about the whole thing and was about to reply to Lord Derby's last letter in terms which could only have made matters worse. I was able to persuade him not to reply but to allow me to see if I could do something to get the matter dealt with on lines which would not only bring about an amicable solution but might also leave the long friendship unimpaired. I am sure that further correspondence between the principals will only make matters worse.

I do not know whether you are conversant with the whole matter as Lord Derby's letters appear to have been written personally.

My object in writing to you is to ascertain whether you or someone on his Lordship's behalf would see me to discuss the matter and see what can be done.

When Mr Lloyd went to Knowsley he was shown a long draft prepared by Lord Derby. The draft ended:

Now with regard to the Press. Here I am absolutely in the dark. I communicated nothing to the Press, and had no notion that there was anything in the Press until I was telephoned to by the *Evening Standard* to say that Mr Lambton had made a statement and would I comment on it. I said No, and I telephoned to Lord Beaverbrook to beg him to allow nothing to go into his papers with regard to Mr Lambton and myself having parted company.

I was coming up to Knowsley, and when I was at Euston I saw a paragraph in the paper, and a reporter came and asked me to comment on it. I then paid what I hoped would be considered a handsome tribute to Mr Lambton's capabilities. When I was afterwards pressed, the next day, as to why we parted, and when I found there were many rumours about (all untrue) as to the reason, I told the truth, and said it was on the ground of ill health. I am extremely sorry Mr Lambton thinks that that has done him harm. It certainly was the last thing in the world I would wish to do.

Finally, if I could do anything to heal the breach I would do so, though I confess I am both hurt and angry at the way my offer has been treated. If, however, Mr Lambton is ready to admit that his refusal was due to a misunderstanding I might again make my offer. I was quite prepared at the time I made the offer for him to say that, not as a profession but for his own amusement, he wanted to go on training a few horses. I should then have told him that to do so would in no way vitiate the pension I proposed to give him.

Understandably the press made the "sacking" of Lambton into a sensational story, and emphasized the fact that he had served the Stanley family faithfully for more than forty years. However, news-hungry reporters received few morsels from either, and were only able to quote:

"I am not retiring," said Mr Lambton yesterday, "and I shall continue to train horses as a public trainer as soon as I can obtain a suitable training establishment.

I hope to remain at Newmarket if possible. If I cannot obtain a suitable establishment at Newmarket I shall take a place elsewhere."

Mrs Lambton said: "We will be leaving Stanley House before January 1. We cannot give the reasons for the change. In fact, I do not think there are any to give."

Whilst an enquiry at Knowsley evoked: "His Lordship does not wish to say anything about the matter."

Two days before Christmas, George Lambton was presented with a silver salver by the Stanley House staff. He told them:

There are three factors, in the many years that I have been trainer here, of which I have been especially proud. They are the goodwill, the friendship and the efficiency of the men and the boys who have done so much to make a success of the Stable.

We have always been a happy family. Some of you older men must have wondered why I kept silent – but to tell you the truth, I have had neither the strength or the courage to speak to you. It is all too painful and it has nearly broken my heart to break away.

11

Old Men Remember . . .

George Lambton did not let the grass grow under his feet, and in December 1933 it was announced that he had bought Kremlin House, the training establishment occupied by Geoffrey Barling, who shared the stabling with Walter Earl. It was also announced that he would train for Lord Durham and for Señor S. J. Unzue, a wealthy South American bloodstock-breeder.

Misfortune hit Lambton almost immediately the 1934 Flat Season started, for Versicle, whom he fancied greatly for the Lincoln, was involved in an accident when the horse-box taking her to the racecourse crashed into an ambulance near Cambridge. A nurse in the ambulance was killed, an apprentice travelling in the horse-box badly injured, and Versicle scratched from the race.

Many people wondered why George Lambton troubled to set up as a public trainer for the first time in his life when he was over seventy years of age. Perhaps the reason was his determination, and that of his wife Cicely, to pave the way for their son Edward to become a trainer. They both felt that it would be easier for him if they provided him with a "ready-made" training establishment, but at the same time they knew that after a lifetime associated with horses, their existence would be dull if they meekly accepted retirement.

In the 1931 Easter holidays after his first half at Eton, Edward (Teddy) Lambton had fallen off a very moderate filly on the gallops, and smashed his right ankle badly. As a result he missed the entire summer half, with "all the cricket and everything which goes to make a young boy's schooldays happy". Eighteen months later he left Eton, where his greatest claim to fame was to have told all and sundry that Dorigen would win the Lincoln. He kept telephoning the butler at Mesnil Warren to put another pound on her – either for himself or his Eton friends. However his father was furious when he discovered what was happening, and lectured him on the evils of betting. After Dorigen's triumph Edward attempted to mollify his father by buying him a cigarette box with Dorigen's name engraved upon it. When the gift was presented George Lambton merely smiled at his son and remarked: "You crafty little beast." Having left Eton, Edward was sent to Stanley Wootton at Epsom, and in his first season as an amateur he won five races.

When George Lambton began training at Kremlin House, Osgood left Stanley House to stay in his employment. Scarlet Tiger and Versicle were the only horses of merit in the yard, but by midsummer both had broken down, and it was left to the humble six-year-old Pricket to become Lambton's first winner since he became a public trainer when he took races at Kempton and Epsom. However, good fortune now smiled upon him, for Major Dermot and Lady Helen McCalmont, who had fallen out with his cousin "Atty" Persse, asked him to train their horses. At the end of the year he had even greater fortune when M. Marcel Boussac sent him Corrida. Proof that he had not lost his magic touch came during the first month of the 1935 season, when he saddled the winner of the Victoria Cup and the Chester Cup. His owners now included Jack Clayton and the Hon. Mrs Freddie Cripps. The following year he scored even greater triumphs with M. Boussac's Goya II, who won the Gimcrack Stakes at York. Goya II was a brilliant colt whom Lambton trained to finish second in the Two Thousand Guineas and Champion Stakes and to win the St James's Palace Stakes. The colt was much fancied for the Derby but dissipated his chance by failing to settle.

Now that temperatures were beginning to cool in the quarrel between Lord Derby and George Lambton, both men sensed that it was time to offer olive branches. Lambton's tangible gesture took the form of writing *Scapa Flow – A Great Brood Mare* for Lord Derby. The book was printed privately, and Lord Derby wrote to Cicely Lambton:

I send you back George's story with a letter attached. That is for George to see. This is a letter which is not for his eye.

I did not see you at Epsom. I was away on the Friday and I have no chance of seeing you now till Ascot when opportunities for discussing things are few and far between, though I hope George, you, Teddy and Sybil will come to luncheon with me every day. You know where the luncheon room is.

Now for the real reason of this private letter. What George says about my not making any payment to him for it is nonsense and I insist on doing it. I should really not feel that the book was mine unless I did and therefore far from my doing any favour to him he is conferring a favour on me. Let me know privately what you would consider a fair sum for me to give him if he had written it for a perfect stranger.

Now another point, about getting it published. I wonder whether you would undertake this for me. You know about those sort of things and I do not. If you would consent I would leave it entirely to you and everything that you did I should think right and be deeply grateful to you for it. Put in such photographs as you think right and indeed have it in exactly the form in which you would like to see it. You would also know better than I should how many copies to have printed. I do not think it is a book that would interest anybody except just our friends and therefore it would be better to limit the number of copies, of which I would take what I wanted and would give George and you any that you wanted.

These are all matters on which you could speak as an expert and I know nothing about it so will you help me with regard to this.

A year later, in October 1938, Lord and Lady Derby suffered a personal sorrow with the death of their eldest son and heir, Edward Stanley, at the age of forty-four. After serving in the Grenadier Guards for much of the First World War he had been elected MP for the Abercromby division of Liverpool in 1917, becoming the youngest member of the House of Commons. From 1922 he represented the Fylde division of Lancashire and in 1931 was appointed Financial Secretary to the Admiralty. Six months before his death he attained Cabinet rank when he was invited by Mr Neville Chamberlain to become Secretary of State for the Dominions. The best horse to win in his racing colours of "black, white belt and cap" was Quashed, leased to him for her racing career by Lady Barbara Smith. Quashed won the 1935 Oaks and the 1936 Ascot Gold Cup.

In a letter of condolence to Lord Derby after Edward Stanley's death, his great friend Lord Beaverbrook wrote: "you hold the love of the people, and they mourn with you . . ." Within a year Lord Derby, perturbed by news from the South of France, was writing to Beaverbrook asking him if he could find a buyer for Sansovino, his villa at Cannes, which he now felt was superfluous to his requirements, particularly with the clouds of war gathering across Europe.

In March 1940 Cicely Lambton's mother died at The Manor House, Wells, where she had entertained Queen Mary in the first months of the war. After her death Lady Oxford wrote:

Though the furrows in her forehead registered the shadows and sorrows of her life, she was as interested, active and gay when she was a great-grandmother as when I first met her . . . it is not uncommon to find men and women of many talents, great vitality, and the highest intelligence whom we delight to be with, but who leave us with a sense of fatigue. They have taken from us more than we have given; their minds seem to be on tip-toe, and we are not so much stimulated as exhausted by their vitality. Few of us could feel this when we were in the company of Frances Horner. She never extinguished but always helped other lights to shine . . . though a woman of outstanding intellect, she never inflicted it on you, and she often told me that causes left her cold, and how little patience she had with vehement convictions.

With the outbreak of the Second World War, the St Leger and the Doncaster Yearling Sales were cancelled, and although some fixtures were held in the autumn the racing season was brought into disarray. Nevertheless the 1939 season had been very successful for Lord Derby, whose stallions Fairway, Hyperion and Caerleon finished first, second and fourth on the Sires List. Yet the pleasure that this record gave him was far outweighed by his misery that hostilities were again turning Europe into a battlefield, and that ill health prevented him leading an active life. By the summer of 1940, when his colt Lighthouse II started favourite for the wartime Derby at Newmarket and Winston Churchill was inspiring the nation with his "We shall fight them on the beaches . . ." he was even more despondent, particularly concerning the future of the breeding industry, for he realized that breeders would face huge problems if they had no prospect of selling their bloodstock.

Many critics considered it outrageous that racing was permitted at a time when Britain was fighting for her survival, and their criticism reached so great a height that George Lambton felt obliged to make a vigorous defence. In May he wrote to *The Times*:

> Sir, – It requires a man of some moral courage to stand up and take the odium that would be thrown at him of being so lost to any sense of decency that he could give his mind to horse racing while his country is in the throes of such a desperate struggle, but my brother, Lord Durham, although he himself never set foot upon a racecourse during the War [1914–18], wrote a letter to *The Times* setting forth plainly the reasons for continuing racing and showing that the complete stoppage of racing would mean the ruin of an industry in which Britain was supreme. There were letters from the late Lord Rosebery and Lord Derby to the same effect. These carried great weight and had much to do with

changing public opinion, and it was not very long before the Government recognized the true position. . . . One of the arguments used by those who thought that racing should stop was that the men who were fighting in France were strongly opposed to it. I believe this to have been an absolute fallacy. I certainly never met one man of the fighting forces, officer or private, who held that opinion, and I was in constant touch with them. I was frequently asked whether I would show parties of men who were on leave round Lord Derby's stable, more especially men of the overseas forces, Australians, Canadians, New Zealanders, and Americans.

Again on one occasion I went to France to see my brother, General Sir William Lambton, who had been terribly injured and whose life was in great danger. He was in a clearing station, close to Arras and near the firing line. Before I had been in the camp a couple of days I found officers, Tommies, doctors, and nurses all talking and asking me about racing, and the racing and sporting papers were all studied with the greatest interest . . .

I will quote some lines in a leading article in your issue of today: "The courage to go on quietly doing one's job to the very height of capacity and endurance is a courage which the civilian need not be ashamed to range in support of the shining bravery of those who fight for him." My job is racing and I am not ashamed to carry on, and if when we have won this war I have left something for a younger generation to build up again I shall be content. We have in our Labour Minister, Mr Ernest Bevin, a great man and one who is like Mr Lloyd George in 1914, ruthless in his prosecution of the War. So long as limited racing has his sanction those who are in doubt may also be content.

I am, Sir, yours faithfully

GEORGE LAMBTON.

Mesnil Warren, Newmarket, May 29.

This letter largely brought the criticism to a halt.

In the autumn of 1940 Lord Derby was involved in a motorcar accident which left him partially crippled. His right hand was damaged so that he could barely sign letters, and he was finding that he was too bulky and too arthritic to travel far. Knowsley became the centre of his existence, and he seldom left the house. His grand-daughter Priscilla Bullock virtually ran Knowsley and became the "lifeline" upon whom he and his wife depended. When in April 1941 it appeared that she was to be called up, he was desolate, for she helped him in many ways and kept him in touch with the outside world. Lady Derby was also finding that old age was precluding her activities, particularly gardening. Between the wars she had created a magnificent garden at Coworth Park which adjoined Fort Belvedere. She had known the Prince of Wales for many years, and a signed photograph of the Prince had always been prominently displayed in the drawing-room until the Abdication, when it was removed and never seen again. Like Lord Derby she always placed "duty" high on her list of priorities. She was to suffer great personal sorrow, in that her husband and all her children were to die before her. She had loved her thoroughbreds, understood and appreciated the breeding theories of Colonel Vuillier,* and had made a success of her annual yearling sales from the progeny of her mares at Swynford Paddocks. Equally she had adored her gardens and her dogs, but had little interest in either food or drink and seldom altered the proposed menus of her chefs and cooks. By 1940 she too was finding life burdensome and spent most of her life quietly at Knowsley.†

George Lambton always retained the highest respect for Lady Derby, whom he invariably found to be gracious and charming. She may have shunned the limelight of public life, and seemed formal to others, but between her and George Lambton there was always an affection and a rapport based upon a genuine love of thoroughbreds.

George Lambton was also suffering strain in his old age, and not enjoying the austerity of wartime Newmarket. In August 1941 his son John, aged thirty-two, was killed in a flying boat accident at Gibraltar, which brought him the utmost sorrow but strengthened his patriotism. His habit of writing to newspapers became more frequent, and in a letter to *The Times* (17 March) he stated:

> I can imagine no more valuable propaganda for the Axis than "England, starving, has to destroy her valuable bloodstock", and at this time it is not easy for the Axis to find good matter for their propaganda. No one can accuse the members of this Government of being particularly interested in racing, but it is a Government that has the trust and confidence of the Empire, so why cannot these busybodies leave this matter to their discretion.

---

* Colonel J. Vuillier, who managed HH Aga Khan's stud at Marly-la-Ville, and who propounded a system of dosages in thoroughbreds in his book *Les Croisements Rationnels*.

† Lady Derby died in July 1957–the year in which His Highness the Aga Khan and Frank Butters also died.

I must refer shortly to a letter in *The Times* today written by Mr Gilbert Johnstone. He infers that horses are only kept in training to provide a means of betting and to assist the bookmakers to flourish. He is an old friend of mine, but I do not hesitate to tell him that this is a gross libel on many hundreds of his country-men. Eighty per cent of horses, especially steeplechase horses, are kept by people in whom a love of horses and of sport is inherent, as it is in very many thousands of men and women of the British Empire at home and abroad.

In an article in *Country Life* (18 January 1941) he wrote:

In a newspaper recently I saw this paragraph: "Sir Archibald Wavell goes to the Races. General Sir Archibald Wavell spent the afternoon at the Races in Cairo, a racecourse crowd gave him a rousing welcome." So it is evident that this brilliant and success-ful commander does not consider it prejudicial to the successful conduct of the war that he should spend an hour or so of leisure on a racecourse. In this country, however, there is rather a different attitude, and those of us who advocate the importance of the continuation of racing and horse breeding are often met, not with any argument, but with the question: "Do you know there is a war on?" – a phrase which, by the way, has been a godsend to many a jack-in-office! It is not difficult to find a reason for this. Here we are in the throes of the cruellest and most desperate war that has ever been waged; tragedies that break our hearts are occurring by day and by night on the sea, on the land, and in the air, so that it is no wonder that many people look upon the continuation of racing, or indeed of any sport, as heartless and unnecessary.

But there is another side to the question. If racing were stopped altogether, would it increase our output of munitions, or would there be one tragedy less? I say most emphatically "No" but it would throw many people out of work and completely ruin a large number who have all their capital invested in the racing and horse-breeding industry.

For the last few years our politicians, especially those in high places, have had no interest in horse-racing or in the breeding of bloodstock; they do not consider them to be of any national importance, and appear to look upon those connected with them with some contempt. The undoubted supremacy that England has held over the whole world in horse breeding for at least a century is not a matter of pride and satisfaction to them. That people should come from all over the world to buy our horses, and that the export trade is of considerable value, is to them a matter of little importance. These are not idle fancies, but the sober truth. This is a mechanical age; we are fighting a mechanical war. The inventions and devices of mankind are marvellous – almost unbelievable – and these, added to the indomitable courage and skill of our sailors, soldiers and air force and also of our munition workers, will win the war. Mechanical war is brutal, cruel and ruthless, but when it is over we all still look forward to a world of sanity and peace; but that will not easily happen if we become mechanized body and soul, and there is considerable danger of this unless we keep alive the old sports and pastimes for which England has always been famous.

Racing, there is no doubt, is the greatest factor in bringing together people of all classes. The old saying that "On the Turf and under it all men are equal" is a true one, and Bismarck's remark to Disraeli, "So long as you keep your racing in England you will never have a revolution" should be remembered.

The present moment is a dangerous one for those interested in the bloodstock industry. We may be sure that the faddists and those people to whom sport is antipathetic will not lose their opportunities, and they will have to be fought, and fought continuously.

The Stewards of the Jockey Club have been in a difficult position, but I cannot absolve them from all blame, for they have not taken the lead as they should have done. I believe I am correct in saying that with the exception of Lord Ilchester not one member of the Jockey Club nor one leading owner has come into the open and stated boldly that the continuance of racing is a matter of national importance, and that to give up racing would be a national disaster. Lord Harewood I know has done valuable work and has not spared himself, and I believe that but for him and for Mr Ernest Bevin, the Minister of Labour, there would have been no racing at all after the spring of last year. The position in the last war was very different. Many influential men wrote letters to *The Times* and stated the reasons why racing should be carried on. Their statements carried some weight with the politicians and even with those members of the public who knew and cared nothing for the sport, and the opposition soon died down. Something of that sort is what we have wanted and what we want now.

What are the prospects for 1941? No one can view them with any complacency. Owners, trainers and breeders have in the past year been very hardly hit financially. The large class of small owners and breeders, the real lovers of racing and horses, the backbone of the industry, cannot stand much more, and it is not going to be easy to keep racing going. It certainly will not be done by sitting down quietly and waiting to see what will happen. Bad times will have to be faced, perhaps worse than at the present moment: we must be prepared and ready for them with the determination to carry on at all costs so long as there is no interference with the prosecution of the war. That has always been the spirit of England. We must not let sentiment, sorrow and horror get us down – that will do no good to anyone. Anything that for an hour or two can give relaxation and take our thoughts off the war is invaluable. This war, apart altogether from its brutalities, has been a most gloomy one – no military bands, no colour, no life! Incidentally, why has there been no martial music? It is a marvellous tonic both to soldier and civilian.

If the Jockey Club will fight for racing not as a favour but as a right, the public will back them to the limit. I will not reiterate all the arguments for and against racing, but if it is again stopped I am afraid it will mean the ruin of the industry and of thousands of people concerned. They are prepared to put up with hard times, loss of capital and so on, like most people in these days, but not with extinction.

Until the full programmes for future racing are published in the Calendar it is not possible to say what the financial outlook will be for owners, and we must hope that these will be published as soon as possible. I have no doubt that it has not escaped the notice of the Jockey Club that certain racecourses have had, owing to the war, record attendances, record entries, and must have prospered exceedingly, yet there was no increase in the value of their stakes!

The difficulties during the next six months, or perhaps longer, will be great, but I am confident that they will be overcome. There will be many stones thrown at the advocates of racing, but I can look forward to the day when we shall see our King and Queen, who have earned the admiration, respect, and love of the world, once again in the Royal Box at Epsom and Ascot acknowledging the welcome that comes from the hearts of their people.

A year later Lord Derby was writing to him (26 February 1942) from Knowsley:

I am afraid we are not going to get many concessions from Cripps and I think perhaps you are right when you say that racing is in danger. I did not think so but Cripps' speech yesterday shows pretty clearly that no concessions will be made, at all events not publicly though I think somehow we shall be able to get enough racing just to keep us going. Of course, to my mind, perhaps even more serious than the absence of racing is the difficulty of keeping the stud farms going; though I am hopeful that the permission to get men from Ireland may help.

As you know I advocate racing in all its forms but there is no doubt whatever if we take up the cudgels for steeple-chasing, the horses taking part in which consist of a lot of old geldings, we cannot at the same time use what I think is the most important argument, the keeping up of our bloodstock.

I am afraid Cripps' speech yesterday in the House of Commons is not helpful to us from the racing point of view. At the same time from what I heard yesterday from a friend of his he is not so violently opposed to racing as might be thought from what he said.

Big Game won the 1942 Two Thousand Guineas in the colours of King George VI, and Lord Derby commented to Lambton:

I have just heard on the wireless the results of the 2,000. I must say the result is very much what I expected and I am not in the least disappointed at neither of mine winning.

I personally always hoped Watling Street would be the better of the two because more than the other it is my own breeding. I should think The King's is a very good horse and it is certainly a good thing for racing that he should win. I wish however it had been a Hyperion who had won. I am afraid it will mean that Bahram will be the head of the Stallions List this year. Of course the worst of it is however good a stallion he is, the Aga will have no compunction whatever about selling him and to any country whether enemy or not which wants to buy him. As you know I have a very poor opinion of the Aga's patriotism.

However, Watling Street won the New Derby for Lord Derby in midsummer, and Cicely Lambton wrote to congratulate him:

First of all we were *so* delighted about Watling Street and the only sad thing was that you were not here to see him win. It was grand in every way; Lady Alice being here and Ruth and Pris, and if anyone had to beat the King thank goodness it was you! We were so pleased about it.

Then, thank you so very much for our night in London which we both enjoyed. I know I did for I hadn't been away from here for a night for about 6 months. As you say it is impossible to see anything of anyone in those hotels and the noise in the restaurant is impossible. All the same I couldn't have enjoyed my "outing" more and it did George good too. It was so very nice of you.

George Lambton also wrote to Lord Derby concerning Watling Street's Derby victory at Newmarket.

I have had no time to write and congratulate you on Watling Street. It was a most exciting race. No horse could have run gamer, no jockey could have ridden better. It was sad that you were not here to see it. I saw Walter* riding the horse as a hack this morning – it really was a great feat to win The Derby with such a very difficult horse to train. I take my hat off to him.

I sent you a wire to ask for Bevin's address – my daughter Billy has been called-up. I appealed for her to be allowed to stay where she is. She has been in the Civil Defence here since March 1940 as an Ambulance driver. She drove the ambulance all through our blitz here, she is always on duty when the siren goes; she sleeps at the hospital three nights a week . . . besides the war work she is almost indispensable to me here, in the stables and on my stud farm . . . I have never seen anyone work so hard, and without a holiday for three years. I am writing to Bevin but I do not suppose he can or will do anything – I don't think I can carry on without her.

A month later Lord Derby wrote to George Lambton:

I must tell you one thing which I confess has annoyed me. I wonder what you think about it. I am told people think that I no longer have any interest in racing. I cannot think what is at the bottom of that because as you know I take as much as ever I did but naturally under different conditions. In the old days I had Edward and Victoria with me the whole time and I was able to be in more constant touch with racing because I was not as infirm as I am now. I cannot get about now and naturally therefore that

* Walter Earl, appointed trainer to Lord Derby on 1 January 1939.

must take off to a certain extent from one's active interest in racing. I will do anything I can for racing and it does rather hurt one when one hears that Newmarket people say that I have dropped all interest in racing. If you hear it I wish you would contradict it. You know exactly what the position is and I am sure sympathize with me and know it is my misfortune and not my fault that I am not able to do as much racing now as I used to. However, luckily the enthusiasm I used to have and also the youth I used to have, have gone to my grandchildren and you would not find any four people more keen about racing than John, Richard, Ruth and Priscilla, and I must leave it to them to do the actual racing for the future, though I will do as you know anything in my power to help the sport.

But there is one thing I do wish and that is that people would give up this extremely optimistic view that they have of the future of racing. It cannot anyhow under the best circumstances be anything but a shadow of its former self, but you may be sure as long as the shadow remains I will do all I can to help racing.

You really are a wonder the way you keep things going just as if you were 30 years younger. Give my love to Cicely. I wish I thought there was a chance of seeing you.

At the end of August Lord Derby's younger brother died, and he wrote:

Thanks for your sympathy too about Brother Bill. It is rather a tragedy to think he has gone – 13 years younger than myself. The doctor had passed him all sound in the morning; he went out in the garden after luncheon to do some weeding and when he didn't come in for tea they went out and found him dead. A happy end, very like my Father's. There really is not much to live for nowadays.

I feel very like you, but with half your energy. I am a limp rag and this weather gets one down so completely; nothing but rain, rain, rain every day. We have had 3 warm days since last May.

I do not know what to think of things generally. The Boche seems always to be just a little ahead of us. We do not seem to have any good Generals, and what I think is so terrible at the present moment is that if a man makes the slightest mistake he is got rid of. It destroys all the confidence of the Army and of the country in any of our Generals. The Germans give a man a second chance, and I think they are very wise to do so.

Now with regard to racing. It is very interesting what you say about Watling Street, and I am hopeful that he may run well next week. I cannot get down myself. It is not that I am so busy, although I have got a certain amount to do, but I do not want to give rise to any sort of talk here about wasting petrol. People are only too ready to make mischief in that direction on the slightest excuse; and in addition to that I really am now so lame that I am able to get about very little, and to sit in the Stand on a wet day without being able to walk about at all does not appeal to me. . . .

They tell me, I am glad to say, that I have got a good lot of yearlings. They will go down south in about a week's time. I wonder what is in store for them in the way of racing. Personally as you know I am usually a pessimist, and I believe myself we have had more racing this year than we shall see next year.

What I am thinking of doing is waiting till the racing season is over and then going down to Newmarket for 2 or 3 days and go round the whole place, seeing whatever animals I have still got left and talk over what I shall sell at the December Sales. Personally I think it is best to cut down the number as much as possible as I am sure in addition to difficulties about having little racing there will also be great difficulties about forage, labour, etc. . . .

Richard is much better but he will always have one leg a little shorter than the other – I do not think very noticeable, but still the shortening will be there. John is all right now and is going back to the Service Battalion which delights him, but I cannot say I am altogether as pleased as he is about it. What is your Teddy doing? I have not heard of him for some time. Has he gone out yet or has that beastly moment of saying goodbye still got to come to you?

The relationship of Lord Derby with George Lambton now seemed to have returned to its zenith, and in November he wrote:

You do not know how much I appreciated your letter and for many reasons. I hear so little from outside sources at Newmarket or indeed from anywhere that what I do get I appreciate very much indeed. . . .

I agree with you racing is going to go through a difficult time but there is one thing that I am certain of and that is there is more genuine appreciation of racing from The King than there has ever been before. There has been a Royal Visit up here and I had one or two talks with him and I am glad to say that his outlook on racing is I think a very different thing to what it was a short time back. I think also the Ministerial outlook is much better.

I wish I could find another stallion to follow on to Fairway and Hyperion. They are both doing marvellously well but of course they cannot go on for ever and like me they are beginning to show signs of old age especially Fairway who has been a wonderful old horse.

But what racing will be after the War is very difficult to foresee: so many of our old friends have gone and those who are left perhaps looking on racing from rather a different angle to what you and I used to look at it. Still there it is. Love of racing evidently still exists and I am very hopeful of the future though I do not think I personally shall see much of it after the War. I am terribly infirm at the present moment and my rheumatism gets worse and worse every day. The younger generation is I think just as keen as I was in my younger days, and probably know more about it than I ever did. Of course Ruth and Priscilla are racing mad though in the latter's case it does not prevent her doing a full day's work as a Wren.

As I tell you my rheumatism gets worse and worse and I am really quite helpless now. It is as much as I can do to get out of a chair and it is pain and grief to sit down in one. However I suppose I ought not to complain and I am very lucky at my age to get off so lightly. . . .

I do not hear much from France and although they have been free till now I should think all my animals that I left there are now in the possession of the Boche. Of course you know poor St Alary is dead. He had really been very ill for the past 2 or 3 years. I shall miss him very much in the future as he was so thoroughly pro-English and looked upon all racing matters from what I may call a British point of view.

I do not know any of the younger lot in France. I do not even know them here. Do tell me what you think of them. I rather like what I hear about Rank.* I should think he is a rough diamond but still keen about racing and very helpful in any matters connected with it.

I wish from time to time you would give me your views, in confidence, of people who are coming new into the racing world.

* Mr J. V. Rank (1881–1952), who had bought the Druid's Lodge training stables in 1935 and had owned such top-class horses as Epigram and Scottish Union. In 1943 his filly Why Hurry won The Oaks.

Lord Derby follows up with three more letters. On 8 December:

> Many thanks for your letter which I was delighted to get. As you know I had meant to come up to London this week but really now what with the difficulties of travelling and acute rheumatism I am very glad I decided not to do so.
>
> I am afraid we are in for a very tough time in North Africa. Still I hope and believe all will go well but why on earth they should have decided to ring the church bells last Sunday week beats me. Doing so was an invitation to things to go wrong.
>
> As you say the Sales went very well indeed, much better than one could have expected but I agree with Harry Rosebery and I think there is another side to the picture and the Government may think because of these Sales racing is so prosperous and they are not going to make things any easier for us in the future when it comes to a question of taxation.

On 21 January 1943:

> I am not really alarmed about the future of racing except from the point of view of Labour and that I think is going to be extremely difficult and will get more difficult every day. Still I daresay we shall manage to worry through somehow.
>
> I am just going in now to Liverpool to have a talk with the Sports Editor of the *Daily Mail* who from his writing would appear to be a sensible sort of fellow. But life is very tiring at the present moment and I confess that even if there were a race meeting in the Park I do not know that I should have energy enough to go to it.
>
> I hear satisfactory accounts of the horses but I do not appear to have another Hyperion nor am I likely to do so. There is tremendous competition for nominations to him and also to Fairway but I am limiting the latter to very few mares as he is getting an old horse now.
>
> I hear really no racing news whatever. As I say I may go south next week. I cannot make up my mind. I would like to go for some things but the journey now seems to be cold and lengthy so I very likely shall not go. If I do I will let you know and perhaps you could come up and see me and have luncheon with me at Claridges.

Again on 24 March:

> I am so very glad to get your letter. It was nice of you to write and

especially was it nice of you to say what you do about Priscilla. I must say she is one of the best sort in the world which is everything to both Alice and me and she never complains though I feel it is a dull life for a girl but she seems very happy and I think is so.

Have you heard anything of your Teddy lately? John is out in Tunisia in the middle of the fighting which naturally makes one very anxious. I personally am very well in myself but hopelessly lame, not only from rheumatism but also from a bad toe which is extremely uncomfortable and painful.

We are expecting the Woods here this afternoon. You are quite right in what you say about him. He is a first class fellow. He is going back to his Regiment in Windsor at the end of the week but I am very much afraid it will mean his going out again before very long. I shall try and persuade him to stay at home and do a little House of Commons work. We want fellows like him here now as really some of the fellows who are in Parliament seem only to exist there with a view of putting questions to embarrass the Government.

I hear occasionally about you and Cicely. I hope you are both well though I did hear that you had been very seedy.

I hope things are going well in the war but I do not quite like the news today. I firmly believe everything will come right in the end but I am afraid there is a hard road in front of us.

George Lambton wrote regarding the 1943 One Thousand Guineas in which Lord Derby's Herringbone defeated Lord Rosebery's Ribbon:

The 1000 guineas was a beautiful race, both fillies running very gamely and straight. I thought once that Herringbone was going to win cleverly but Ribbon hung on so well that I should say that Herringbone was all out at the finish, but Ribbon had a very hard race. Wragg rode beautifully. . . . Frank Butters tells me that Gordon Richards still says that he will win The Derby, that he[*] did not like blinkers and that he rode him the wrong way. I doubt all this. . . .

On the death of the Duke of Portland, for whom he had trained several horses, Lambton wrote:

It is sad the end of the perfect life – but I am thankful that he was

[*] The Aga Khan's Nasrullah.

spared a long illness which is what all old people have to pray for – what will happen to Welbeck! "Sunny" was very keen about Racing to the last. I wish he could have won his last race instead of being second. We have suddenly gone back to Winter, most disagreeable, but with a good rain which we wanted badly. The King was here on Wednesday. I believe he is quite keen on racing. He went to see all your stallions . . . what with those Poles and the American strike it does not seem hopeful for the better world about which we hear so much. I have no doubt, that the Russians did murder a lot of Poles but what is the use of making trouble now. They have always been impossible people, although some of their individuals are very attractive . . . Sefton said the Stewards did not agree with the Report that Amateur races should be encouraged – they did not consider them necessary. I think in these days they are the very people most necessary to encourage.

Lord Derby replied on 31 May:

I cannot tell you how grateful I am to you for your letter. It is just the sort of information that I do not get from anybody else and I am afraid any question of a visit to Newmarket, at all events at present, is impossible. It looks to me as if Wragg had really snatched the One Thousand from Ribbon. He seems to have ridden a beautiful race as I think he generally does. . . .

I do not think Herringbone will ever be considered a really first class mare. At the same time she is very useful and very game and really this year is what Watling Street was to me last year. I am very glad she should have won as it justifies my having brought in my French stud. I always thought that might turn out trumps.

As far as I can make out I do not think I have got a good colt.

The racing world seems to be going along quite evenly and well. I should think Hugh Sefton has been a really good steward. Thank God it was not his father. I am very fond of Hugh. I could not stand Osbert and I disliked his father even more.

I find plenty to do here but I am getting very lazy about doing anything. This week we have got the Duchess of Gloucester coming up for various things. I must say the Royal Family are very good the way they work. . . .

With regard to my own family, John has I am glad to say come so far safely through the Tunisian fighting. The battalion though has been almost wiped out. The whole thing is very horrible and one feels very much if it had not been for Clemenceau and Lloyd George we might in the last Peace have made it practically

impossible for another War to have taken place. I only hope there
will be no weakness shown when we make Peace this time but I
am afraid that Peace won't come till after we have lost a good
many more lives.

I do hope you have got good news of Teddy. Where is he and
what is he doing? Do let me know. All those sort of things about
my friends and their children do interest me very much. I am
quite well in myself, at the same time fearfully infirm with this
beastly rheumatism.

In the autumn George Lambton congratulated Lord Derby on a
speech, and received a reply:

I am glad you approved of what I said but I really do not know
what I did say because it was an unprepared speech and I have not
seen any account of it but I agree with you that it is no use
carrying on bitterness when the war is over if we can possibly
avoid it. What we have got to do is to stop any chance of the
Germans making a renewed attempt against us.

He continued his letter by remarking on the success of the Allied
invasion of Italy, but admitted to having reservations:

Things, as you say, are going well, but I think people are taking a
great deal too much for granted at the present moment and it will
be some time before one can really see the end of this trouble. I
give it another two years myself. Of course, I am not quite sure
that I agree with this "unconditional surrender" policy. You
don't give people the chance of getting out of their trouble.
However there it is. I hope we shall not make the same mess of
the Peace that we did after the last War. That was entirely due to
the French and curiously enough more to Foch and Clemenceau
than to the French nation. I saw a good bit of what was going on
then. I wish we had had Winston in charge then. I think things
would have been different.

I am not going down to Newmarket at all but I am going down
to London in the middle of September to preside at a Pilgrim
luncheon to Wavell. I think I shall take the opportunity of having
two or three days in London and of course it is just possible I
might go down to Newmarket for a couple of days but not in a
race week.

Alice I think thoroughly enjoyed her visit to Newmarket but
unfortunately got rather laid up by overdoing everything. She is I

hope all right again now but she has been quite seedy for the last ten days since she got back.

I was very pleased naturally with Herringbone's win* but it was quite unexpected. As you know I did not go down there. I never go racing now. If I did it would be so liable to misconstruction here that it is better to stay away especially as I am now so hopelessly crippled with rheumatism, and the actual racing would give me very little encouragement. I shall try and come down to Newmarket however some time later just to see the horses. . . .

I am afraid my two year olds are not really much good. If it was not war time there would probably be plenty of little races they could have picked up but, as it is, there is nothing that they are good enough to win.

During the war years George Lambton continued to train with considerable success. In 1940 he had forty horses in his stables at Kremlin House (whilst Lord Derby had twenty-seven with Walter Earl at Stanley House) and in 1941 won the Lincolnshire Handicap with Gloaming, owned by Stephen Raphael, and ridden by young D. V. Dick. Three years later, despite the difficulties imposed by the war, he still had thirty horses in his yard, with his owners including Lord Fitzwilliam, Sir Richard Sykes, Mr Martin Benson, Mr H. E. Morriss and Major Dermot McCalmont, for whom he had trained Lapel to win the 1938 Irish One Thousand Guineas. Triumvir, Sir Edward and Golden Cloud were winning more than their fair share of races, and Golden Cloud, whom he had astutely bought for a paltry 80 guineas, was to become one of the best sprinters in the country and ultimately a very successful stallion.

Lord Derby's thirty-three horses in training in 1944 included Garden Path, Borealis, All Moonshine, High Peak and Sun Stream, who was to give him his final Classic victories when she won the 1945 One Thousand Guineas and Oaks. During the war years his French bloodstock, including two top-class colts, Nepenthe and Arcot, passed into the hands of his manager, the Marquis de Saint Sauveur, to avoid confiscation by the Germans, and it was in his colours that they raced.

Early in the New Year Lord Derby told George Lambton:

I hear of you from time to time through Ruth. She and Priscilla

* The St Leger.

and Alice are as keen about racing as ever they were and so are John and Richard. The former is now in Italy, but I am afraid it will be a long time before Richard is fit for foreign service. It was a terrible motor accident that he had but in a way it is a blessing in disguise as it will keep him I hope in comparative safety. I am afraid there is going to be some very hard fighting in Italy. I hope you have good news of Teddy.

It is very interesting what you say about the amount we owe to the jockeys we have had but I also feel a great debt of gratitude to you. It is more than I can ever repay. You made the Stable: Walter Alston made the Stud though there again you really laid the foundations.

I think I have got a fair lot of yearlings but nothing out of the way. I wish I could draw on my resources in France as I believe I had some very useful animals there. Certain I have got some good mares but I do not suppose I shall ever see any of them again though so far the Germans have not taken them. . . .

I wish I thought there was a Grand National coming on at which you would be coming up here. I am afraid that must be postponed certainly for this year and probably for two or three years more.

Hugh Sefton is living up here now. He is I am glad to say taking a great interest in local matters. He is giving up being Senior Steward and I think he is rather worried and I do not wonder, at what is going to happen now. Hanmer becomes Senior Steward and although he is a very nice fellow he is certainly not capable of standing up to the Government, and they will want standing up to, though as a matter of fact he has got a firm friend I think in Morrison who has stayed here on one or two occasions and is I think determined to help racing as much as he possibly can.

John is now out of the line – at least we think so. I hope it is true because they have had an awful time there and have lost very heavily. People have been talking as if the war was over whereas, as Oliver writes to me, he is afraid the worst part has still got to come.

So sorry you yourself are not too well. It is this weather. We never seem to get two days alike and I myself am suffering very much from rheumatism, in fact, I cannot get about at all. . . .

I am glad you think well of what you hear of my yearlings. Bunty seems very enthusiastic about them and I hope I have really got one or two good ones. I have got a circular about William of Valence and I intend to take a share. He is so extraordinarily well bred and although there is a Chaucer in his pedigree it is really so far off as not to prevent my using him for mares descended from Chaucer. It really is almost impossible to get any stallion now without blood of this Stud in his pedigree.

On 6 April George Lambton wrote to congratulate Lord Derby on his birthday:

I was glad to see that you reached your 79th year in fairly good health. There was a time when one might have regretted being so old, but I am not sure that is the case in these days. What will be the position of what we call the upper classes in 10 years time!

We were all delighted to hear of John and his M.C. It must be a great joy and pride for all of you; it came as no surprise as we had heard from many sources what splendid work he had done. Thank God for the moment he is away from Anzio.

I have not much news for you. Have not been at all well the last 3 weeks, and by the time I have done with my horses in the morning I am also done for.

I heard that Walter Earl was trying some horses yesterday. I have not seen much of other people's horses but my information is that Happy Landing is not going well, that Frank Butters 3 year olds are not up to classic form – Cinque Foil is said to be the best – also that his two year olds are not first class. Gordon Richards told me that the 3 year olds and two year olds at Beckhampton were not up to the usual standard. I am not sure that he is a good judge of the unfinished article. I have seen Fair Fame going. Her action is splendid, although she looks on the light side. . . .

I hear good accounts of the Bois Roussel 2 year olds. One morning I saw a big chestnut 2 year old going very well in a galop (*sic*) of Stanley House horses. I imagine it was High Peak.

Warm weather and rain have come just in time to save the studs and the land. The price of hay and moderate is fantastic.

Tommy Weston has been riding gallops for me, quite in his old form. He was telephoned for last Friday to return at once, and I should say he won't get any more leave for some time.

I have a nice filly of Richard Sykes by Hyperion-Trustful that probably runs in our first week's racing. He also has a nice Fairway filly out of Jury.

I was glad to see that at last Bevin spoke out strongly about the miners. Lloyd George does not strike me as being a chip off the old block. I don't think his father would have stood for this anarchy in wartime.

Please give my love to Lady Alice and pass on the racing gossip.

Lord Derby replied the same day:

Thank you a thousand times for your letter. I so entirely agree with your sentiments about increasing years. I am sorry to say in my own case it is not only increasing years but decreasing ability to get about, as I am very lame with rheumatism. At the same time I do manage to get about a certain amount. I have still got my same interest in racing that I have always had, but at the same time one cannot have quite the same interest when one is tied by the leg as I am at the present moment as one had when one was able to go racing. . . .

I have had Fred Cripps, who you will remember was Neil's great friend, here for luncheon. We have been talking over old days racing, and while it was delightful to do that it makes one wonder whether the good times will ever come back; and one knows that even if they do there will be some terrible gaps in the list of one's friends. . . .

The only thing that really gives one pleasure nowadays is to think that one's grandchildren are keen about racing, and certainly Ruth and Priscilla are and I think most of the others are as well. Certainly John and Richard are. Again many thanks. Love to you and Cicely. What news have you of Teddy? Good I hope.

On 23 May 1944 Lord Derby wrote to Lambton:

Very many thanks for your letter and for your congratulations about Garden Path.* I should like to have seen the race but travel is now so impossible that neither Alice nor I in our old age would undertake the journey.

I think Garden Path is a good filly and evidently stays well, but I don't really think she is as good as some of those that we had in the past. She is rather highly strung and I am afraid to over-run her, so whether I shall run her in The Derby or not I do not know. I have not made up my mind at all events at present.

I think Sun Stream may develop into a really smashing good mare. At the present moment she is rather excitable, but I think both she and Hydrangea will be very useful additions to the Stud.

Alice is very well and still extraordinarily energetic. At the

* First filly to win the Two Thousand Guineas since Sceptre in 1902.

same time, as with me, though not by any means to the same extent, Anno Domini is beginning to take its toll, and energetic though she is her energy is not quite what it was a year ago; nor could I expect it to be.

As for myself I cannot really walk 50 yards and I have to be wheeled from one room to another.

What news do you have of Teddy? Where is he at the present moment? I suppose he is somewhere in the fighting. John is still out in Italy and is in the middle of all this present fighting. How I wish it would all end.

I expect Cicely is as energetic and as hardworking as ever. Give her my love.

George Lambton, who spent much of his time reading novels provided by the Times Book Club, and by playing bezique and cribbage, replied:

My dear Eddie,
Although I have not written to you, I have often thought about you. For the last few weeks I have been so ill I have no energy for anything. I am now in the hands of a new doctor Col. MacManus. This may interest Lady Alice! He says he will put me on my legs.

I read the other day that you announced your intention of retiring from any more business but privately I hear that except for your legs you are in fine form.

I have seen nothing of any racehorses lately but the last time I was out I saw Borealis galop. He has beautiful action.

Cecil Rochfort has returned from his honeymoon looking well I am told.

War news looks good but there is much country to get over. Teddy writes in good spirits from Italy. Does not think the Germans will do much fighting over there.

Lord Derby replied on 12 August:

I was sorry to hear that you had not been any too well. I hope nothing much wrong. I hear from many people you are working just as hard as ever and it is rather disappointing that with all this hard work there is now very little that you can run horses for. Although some people keep on thinking and saying that the end of the war is near at hand I myself don't see it and cannot think that we shall see peace this year.

I wish I thought I was going to get down to Newmarket but I

do not see the possibility of doing so. In the first place I now, as I told you, can hardly walk and everybody tells me travelling is so uncomfortable that I do not like trying it.

It is rather terrible, and I am sure you feel it as much as I do, the way old names are dropping out of racing and although some of the newcomers are very nice fellows they do not carry on the traditions which the old ones did. I am glad young Fitzwilliam is apparently keen about racing. I am still more pleased that in my own family there is still great enthusiasm for racing and also a great interest in the breeding which is even more important.

John is here at the present moment laid up but not bad and getting better every day. It is the result of the dysentery he had.

Early in the year 1945, which was to see the death of George Lambton, the great trainer wrote to congratulate Lord Derby on his son's political success:

You and Lady Alice must be very pleased at Oliver's great success in the Colonial debate. He has had so many hopeless jobs to tackle in the past that it makes his triumph all the more delightful . . . I have not been out of my room for months and do not know that I ever shall until I am carried out . . . this is the first letter I have written for ages.

Lord Derby commented in reply:

It was nice of you to write as you have done to me about Oliver. I think Oliver has made a great success of his new Office.★ It is the first Office he has really been happy in and I must say it is delightful to feel that not only is he happy himself but those with whom he has to deal seem to be equally pleased with him. . . .

I am so glad you have got a good foal by Fairway. People all crack up Hyperion but I personally am convinced that Fairway is the best stallion I ever had or shall have.

The family generally remain as keen about racing as ever. It is one occupation that really interests Alice and the rest of the family are the same. It is good to think that the family love of racing will be carried on for several generations.

I hope this war will now soon be over and then there will be the release of petrol which will enable me to motor over and see you.

Give my love to Cicely.

★ Colonial Secretary.

By midsummer it was evident that George Lambton's death was imminent, and he was far too ill to see Golden Cloud, ridden by Michael Beary, win at Windsor early in June. On 21 July Cicely wrote to Lord Derby:

> George has been very ill really for a long time . . . he was anxious to get everything fixed-up for Teddy to take over and he asked the Stewards a little while ago if he could relinquish his licence and if they would grant it to Teddy. It was only about ten days ago that George began to go down very rapidly up until then he had been able to see people and quite enjoy a lot of things . . . his keen interest in racing and everything never flagged and his brain and his memory better than all of ours put together! . . . I have got a very good nurse who is devoted to him and who has been with us since last October. It was very sweet of you saying that you would come and see him, and I do appreciate it so much and so does he, but it would be dreadfully tiring for you and may be no use, as we are really just waiting for him to be at rest.

Lord Derby answered the letter two days later:

> Very many thanks for your letter though it distresses me very much to get it. I feel that you, in your letter, hold out little hope of a complete recovery for George and all I feel I can pray for is that he may suffer no pain. He has evidently prepared himself for the end that comes to all of us and which has come appreciably nearer in the last few weeks.
>
> I am very glad that the Stewards should have seen their way to give Teddy a temporary licence as I know what pleasure that must have given to George. Of course it would be impossible for them, as long as he is in the Army, to give the boy anything more than a temporary licence, but I hope it may grow into a permanent one although I cannot help feeling that the permanent one should go to you who have been so wonderfully brave and helpful to George for a very long time.
>
> You must let me know if there is any way that I can help.

George Lambton died on the morning of 23 July. Cicely sent Lord Derby a telegram: "George died this morning very peacefully – Cicely." Lord Derby immediately acknowledged the news in a telegram:

> Just heard the very sad news. Not unprepared for it but still at the

same time shall feel George's loss very acutely. Do let me know anything you have to communicate about the funeral though I am afraid very doubtful if I shall be able to come.

Alice joins with me in sending you our most sincere sympathy. He was one of the oldest friends of both of us.

The telegram was followed by a letter to Cicely:

What can I possibly say to you? Nothing I know that can bring you consolation but the one thing that must console you for your great loss is the fact that for so many years you did everything in the world to help George.

I wish his licence to train could have been continued to you as you certainly thoroughly deserved it.

I should much like to have come down to you today but it is not possible. I have got a round of semi-official visits that have been arranged some time and which I really cannot get out of or even alter, but you will know how much I feel for you and how very deeply I feel George's death.

If there is anything I can do to help you do let me know.

Cicely Lambton replied:

. . . I wanted to write a little letter to you for I know how much George's death must mean to you and to Lady Alice who were his oldest and greatest friends. For myself it seems the end – but I know that I have got to struggle on to help the children and especially Teddy who has a hard task ahead of him. I have a great deal to be thankful for – to have had that wonderful companion for so long . . . I am glad that he was not here to see what he would have thought the débâcle of the Country. He was very worried over the election, for as you know his brain was so acute and so active up to the very last.

George Lambton's funeral took place at All Saints, Newmarket, on 26 July. His estate was proved at £87,552 and in his will, made in September 1939, he left to Cicely "All my plate, plated articles, ·linen, glass, china, books, pictures, prints, furniture, horses, motor cars, jewellery, and other articles of personal or domestic or household use or ornament, and garden effects free of duty." He also left her a legacy of £2,000 and gave her a life interest in the income from his estate. By a codicil to his Will made in January 1945: "I give, devise and bequeath to my wife absolutely all my bloodstock whether in training or at Stud and also my freehold dwelling house known as Mesnil Warren, Newmarket." The freeholds of Kremlin House and the Moreton Stud were left to Teddy, and the balance of his estate divided two sixths to Teddy, one sixth to John, one sixth to his daughter Anne Katherine Swynford, and two sixths to his daughter Sybil Frances Mary Diadem.★ Curiously there was no deletion of the one-sixth share left to John, who had been killed in 1941. Teddy had been serving in the Middle East in the Royal Horse Guards whilst Anne (Nancy), a Persian scholar and brilliant linguist, was attached to the British Legation in Tehran, where she remained for much of the war.

George and Cicely had been married for thirty-seven years and had proved that two apparent diametrical opposites, the sport of horse racing and the appreciation of art, could be brought into unison. They were immensely happy, and publicly George would support Cicely through thick and thin, although he might privately reprimand her, usually ending up with, "Oh, bosh, woman."

Shortly after George Lambton's death, Cicely† wrote to Lord Derby:

> I want to ask you something which will be a great help to me. Will you let me remain on the list of Hyperion and Fairway because George has left all his bloodstock to me and I am keeping on the Stud.‡ Of course I do not expect the same generous terms you gave to George but I would be awfully grateful if I can have the nominations as he did but at the ordinary fees.

Lord Derby replied (25 August):

> Many thanks for your letter. What I am doing now is only what I did during George's lifetime and which I think he approved of, which was that I did not definitely give any nominations to my stallions till nearer the time of covering. Of course too every year I have to reduce a few owing to stallions getting so much older and that is why I cannot make you a definite promise now to give you a nomination.

★ At the age of forty-one Sybil was to be killed when she fell from her horse, Canuto, at the Brocklesby Point-to-Point in 1962. Her husband, Major W. Jessop, was Master of the South Wold Hunt.

† Cicely Lambton died at Christmas 1972.

‡ The Moreton Stud, on the Fordham Road, had been created by George Lambton in the early 1920s. He kept his own mares on the 200-acre stud, and ultimately stood Mr Jinks as the resident stallion.

I am glad to see Teddy is getting some winners but I cannot help feeling that the winners ought all to be put down to you.

Lord Derby outlived George Lambton by two and a half years, and died at Knowsley at 2 am on 4 February 1948. *The Times* printed a short notice the following day:

LORD DERBY DEAD
Passing of a Great Englishman

We announce with great regret that Lord Derby died at 2 am yesterday at his home in Lancashire at the age of 82. He had been suffering from a bronchial cold for a day or two, and although he was slightly better on Tuesday night he took a turn for the worse in the middle of the night when his heart began to fail and he died in his sleep. His grandson and heir, Lord Stanley, and Lady Derby were present.

His funeral took place at Knowsley, with memorial services being held in Liverpool Cathedral, Manchester Cathedral, Wellington School Chapel and All Saints, Newmarket, where George Lambton had been a Warden for so many years.

Throughout his long life, Lord Derby's strong but sympathetic character, which was combined with an admirable "John Bull" outlook, brought him deserved popularity and prestige, thus making his multitudinous and onerous public duties easier to perform. In the world of horse racing his memory will never fade, for he left an indelible mark on the thoroughbred breeding industry. Consequently it was not surprising that shortly after his death a letter appeared in *The Times* claiming that in his Obituary fuller justice was done to the success of the House of Stanley in the breeding of horses than to its achievements in the production of statesmen and rulers.

INDEX